The Making of a Romantic Icon

The Religious Context of Friedrich Overbeck's *Italia und Germania*

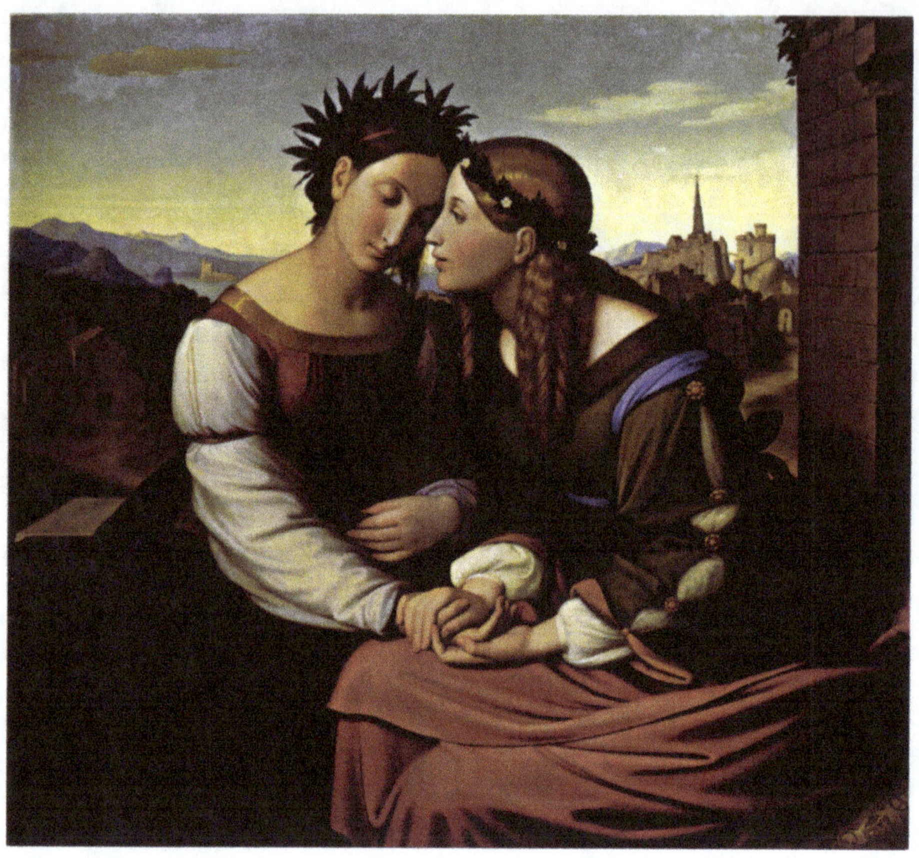

Fig. I. Friedrich Overbeck. *Italia und Germania.* (1811/20). Oil on canvas. 94.4 × 194.7 cm. Unsigned. Munich, Bayerische Staatsgemäldesammlungen, Inv. No. WAF 755.

The Making of a Romantic Icon

The Religious Context of Friedrich Overbeck's *Italia und Germania*

LIONEL GOSSMAN

American Philosophical Society
Philadelphia • 2007

Transactions of the
American Philosophical Society
Held at Philadelphia
For Promoting Useful Knowledge
Volume 97, Part 5

ISBN: 978-0-87169-975-6

Library of Congress Cataloging-in-Publication Data

Gossman, Lionel.
The making of a romantic icon : the religious context of Friedrich Overbeck's Italia und Germania / by Lionel Gossman.
p. cm. — (Transactions of the American Philosophical Society held at Philadelphia for promoting useful knowledge ; v. 97, pt. 5)
Includes bibliographical references and index.
ISBN 978-0-87169-975-6
1. Overbeck, Johann Friedrich, 1789-1869. Italia and Germania. 2. Overbeck, Johann Friedrich, 1789-1869—Criticism and interpretation. 3. Christian art and symbolism—Germany—Modern period, 1500- 4. Romanticism in art—Germany. I. Title.

ND588.O9G67 2007
759.3—dc22 2007040427

Design and Typesetting by
International Graphics Services.

Printed in the United States of America by Hamilton Printing.

I

In June 1855, the German painter Johann Friedrich Overbeck set out from Rome on a journey to his native land. He was sixty-six years old and was leaving the eternal city for only the second time since settling there in 1810, at the age of nineteen, with his band of rebels from the Vienna Academy, the so-called *Lukasbrüder* or Brothers of St. Luke. The brotherhood had disintegrated, its original members having drifted away or died. Even the larger "Nazarene" school of painters, which had grown up around it, inspired by the brothers' preraphaelist artistic principles and their goal of rededicating art to the service of "Truth" (i.e., for them, the truth of revealed religion) instead of the vain pleasures of the rich and powerful, had long been eclipsed by newer, very different artistic movements. Once hailed throughout Europe – in England, they were described in the *Art Journal* in 1839 as "assuredly the greatest artists of Europe" and in France, the author of an open letter to Victor Hugo in the *Revue des Deux Mondes*, proclaimed Germany, thanks to them, "la patrie de l'art régénéré, la seconde Italie de l'Europe moderne" – the Nazarenes had quite rapidly fallen out of favor.[1] By mid-century, most of them had left Rome and returned to Germany. Some held prestigious positions as directors of the very art academies whose teaching they had once spurned. Overbeck alone had resisted all invitations to return to Germany as well as all the newer movements in painting and had remained steadfastly faithful – to the detriment, it has been said, of his art – to the original artistic and religious impetus and inspiration of the *Lukasbund*. "Mir ist die Kunst gleichsam eine Harfe Davids, auf der ich allerzeit Psalmen möchte ertönen lassen zum Lobe des Herrn," he

[1]See my "Unwilling Moderns: The Nazarene Painters of the Nineteenth Century," www.19thc-artworldwide.org, fall 2003, pp. 3-5. On the Nazarenes' fall from favor in Germany, see the excellent, rarely cited article by W. Neuss, "Das Wesen der Nazarenerkunst und ihre Bedeutung für die deutsche Kunst des 19. Jahrhunderts," *Kunstwissenschaftliches Jahrbuch der Görresgesellschaft* (Augsburg: Benno Filser Verlag), 1 (1928): 62-86; also note 115. A century of neglect was followed by a modest revival of interest in the Nazarenes in the late 1920s and a much more vigorous revival in the 1970s. There is now a substantial literature on them in German, as well as a small body of scholarship in English, beginning with the pioneering study of Keith Andrews (1964) – the first since the out-of-date but still valuable 1882 study by J. Bevington Atkinson, a contemporary who had frequented Overbeck's studio in Rome for over twenty years (see note 20 below) – and culminating in the recent work of Mitchell B. Frank. See Appendix.

wrote in a commentary on one of the cartoons for his painting of "The Seven Sacraments" (1847-59).[2]

In 1855, the Italian railway network was still not complete. The journey north from Rome was covered, as it had been in 1810, by *vetturino*. When he finally boarded a train in Milan, it was thus Overbeck's first experience of modern travel. As the train emerged from a tunnel on the line to Como, his biographer Margaret Howitt relates, the nervous artist, clutching his little dog, remarked to his traveling companion: "Let us pray for the Jews." Howitt obligingly explains this odd remembrance of the Good Friday prayer "Oremus et pro perfidis Judaeis." ["Let us pray also for the unbelieving Jews."] It seems that in October 1848 a "Jewish gentleman from Ancona, by the name of Ascoli," had visited Overbeck's studio in Rome and after admiring the artist's work, encouraged him to make a trip home to Germany with assurances that travel had vastly improved thanks to the new railways. The following spring Ascoli had sent him an overview of the lines already in operation and of their projected extension to Rome. "The painter," we are told, "foresaw at the time no chance of ever making use of the new railway since he thought that he had only one more journey to make: the journey to eternity. So he replied to his well-meaning benefactor that he knew of no other way of thanking him than by begging the Lord, who is the source of all that is good, to lead him on the way of truth and life so that they might both reach their eternal homeland together." Now that he was in fact finally making use of the new means of transportation urged on him by Ascoli, Howitt concludes, Overbeck "remembered his indebtedness to the obliging Jew and prayed for him with all his heart."[3]

That this curious anecdote might not be irrelevant to an understanding of one of the artist's best-known paintings is the intuition for which I attempt to provide in this essay some supporting evidence through a broad contextualisation of the work's conception and earlier stages.

---

[2]"Art for me is like a harp of David on which I would like endlessly to play psalms in praise of the Lord" (quoted in Margaret Howitt, *Friedrich Overbeck. Sein Leben und Schaffen*, Franz Binder, ed. [Freiburg: Herder, 1886; rprt. Bern: Herbert Lang, 1971], 2 vols., 2:315). All translations in the text and footnotes, unless stated otherwise, are by L.G.

[3]Howitt, 2:228.

II

Commissioned by the Frankfurt art dealer Friedrich Wenner, a generous supporter of German artists, during a visit he paid to Rome in 1815,[4] Overbeck's *Italia und Germania* **(Fig. I, frontispiece)** was acquired by Ludwig I of Bavaria in 1833 and publicly exhibited at the newly opened Neue Pinakothek in Munich in 1853. Like Mignon's celebrated lines in Goethe's novel *Wilhelm Meisters Lehrjahre* – "Kennst du das Land wo die Zitronen blühen?" – it immediately became an emblem for the educated German middle classes not only of the longstanding love of the nation's poets and artists for Italy, but of their own "Sehnsucht nach Italien." Though Overbeck did not complete the painting until 1828, preliminary drawings for it, on which Wenner no doubt based his commission for an oil painting, date from 1811-1815. The title *Italia und Germania* was suggested by the painter himself as it neared completion. Wenner must have asked him what title to give the painting and Overbeck characteristically explained his suggestion at some length. (Overbeck was much given to verbal explanations of works of art: The elaborate program he supplied to accompany one of his best-known works, *Der Triumph der Religion in den Künsten*, commissioned by the Städelsches Kunstinstitut in Frankfurt am Main, provoked a good deal of negative comment concerning the artistic inadequacy of painting that requires lengthy textual explanation.)

> As far as the further development of the picture's underlying idea is concerned, it will not surprise you that the two young brides [of fifteen years ago] have grown into a couple of dignified women. These two women are *Germania* and *Italia*. For at a later stage in the development of the picture the need arose to give a more precise meaning to the vague concept of my youthful years. The frequently asked question – "What does the picture actually represent?" – itself required that such a meaning be provided. As to why I in fact selected the idea of Germania and Italia, my situation as a German artist here in Italy provides an explanation. On the one hand, these two elements [Germany and Italy] face each other, to some extent, like strangers, but

[4]Howitt, I:486-87.

> on the other hand it is and always will be my task to unite them, at least in the visible form of my work. And that is why I imagine them here as joined in a beautiful and deeply felt friendship. On the one hand, the memory of my homeland, imprinted ineradicably on my soul; on the other, the charm of all that is splendid and beautiful. These two things are what I gratefully enjoy at the present time, both together, not separate and exclusive of each other but united in my mind in harmony and mutual respect. Finally, if the theme had to be expressed more generally, what is intended is the longing that always draws the North to the South, to its art, its natural landscape, its poetry. And the two are adorned like brides – both of them, the longing as well as the object of love – because, as ideas, both are constantly being rejuvenated. That is approximately what I can say by way of explanation. But whether that explanation will make my intention clear to others I do not rightly know, for I understand very well that the conception underlying it stems from my particular situation and standpoint. And so, if a title has to be given to it, one could also call the picture simply "Friendship."[5]

As this letter confirms, *Italia und Germania* was neither the original title of the painting nor its original theme. In fact, the preparatory drawings and sketches were all entitled *Sulamith und Maria*. Without questioning the popular and established understanding of *Italia und Germania*, to which Overbeck himself clearly contributed, I would like to consider here what the earlier title might have to tell about the artist's possible intentions – "the vague concept of my youthful years" – and about his own understanding of his work. The very fact that he found it possible to change the title suggests that in his own mind the two allegorical figures represented in the work could accommodate

[5]"Was nun die weitere Ausbildung der dem Bilde zugrunde liegenden Idee anlangt, so wird es Sie wohl überhaupt nicht wundern, dass nach so vielen Jahren aus den beiden Bräuten ein Paar ehrbarer Frauen geworden sind. Die Frauen *Germania* und *Italia*. Es trat nämlich in späterer Zeit der Ausarbeitung natürlich das Bedürfniss ein, der jugendlich unklaren Vorstellung eine bestimmtere Bedeutung unterzulegen, wozu schon die häufigen Fragen: was denn das Bild eigentlich vorstelle? veranlasste. Dass ich nun aber gerade die Idee einer Germania und Italia wählte, darüber gibt mein besonderer Standpunkt hier als *Deutscher in Italien* Aufschluss. Es sind die beiden Elemente gleichsam, die sich allerdings einerseits fremd gegenüberstehen, die aber zu verschmelzen nun einmal meine Aufgabe, wenigstens in der äusseren Form meines Schaffens, ist und bleiben soll, und die ich desshalb hier in schöner inniger Befreundung mir denke. Es ist einerseits die Erinnerung der Heimath, die unverlöschbar dem Gemüthe eingeprägt steht, und andrerseits der Reiz alles des Herrlichen und Schönen. Was ich dankbar in der Gegenwart geniesse, und Beides zusammen, nicht getrennt und einander ausschliessend, sondern in Harmonie gedacht und in gegenseitiger Würdigung. Es ist endlich, wenn es allgemeiner ausgesprochen werden soll, die Sehnsucht gemeint, die den Norden beständig zum Süden hinzieht, nach seiner Kunst, seiner Natur, seiner Poesie; und diess im bräutlichen Schmuck, Beides, die Sehnsucht sowohl als Gegenstand ihrer Liebe, weil Beides als Idee sich fortwährend verjüngt. – Das ist ungefähr, was ich zur Erklärung darüber zu sagen weiss: ob aber diese Erklärung nun auch Andern klar macht, was ich gewollt, weiss ich freilich nicht, da ich wohl einsehe, dass eine Vorstellung zum Grunde liegt, die aus meinem besondern Standpunkt hervorgegangen; und so mag man das Bild denn auch schlechtweg die *Freundschaft* nennen, wenn ihm einmal ein Name gegeben werden soll" (quoted in Howitt, 1:478-79).

a range of meanings.[6] If, in 1829, he characterized the painting as an allegory of the artistic task he had set himself – to unite the Italian and the German artistic traditions – or, more generally, as an allegory of "Friendship," fourteen years earlier, just after receiving the commission from Wenner, he told Ludwig Vogel, one of the original *Lukasbrüder*, that its theme was "earthly love." Wenner, he explained, had commissioned him to work up a drawing of "two brides" that he had originally made for his friend Franz Pforr into a substantial painting and had also commissioned a companion work of similar dimensions. While he was delighted and excited by Wenner's double commission, he was not sure, he confessed to Vogel, what the subject of the companion work should be – unless perhaps a representation of "heavenly love" (such as Saint Catherine and the Christ child, or an angel bringing wreaths of flowers to St. Cecilia and her betrothed) that would complement the representation of "earthly love" in the first painting.[7] Overbeck himself thus allowed that his image of two women could be read in a variety of ways: as a representation of the relation of Germany and Italy, as a representation of friendship in general, or as a representation of profane love, as distinct from, but in his mind probably not unrelated to sacred love.

In the following pages, I propose to explore the religious context out of which the painting now known as *Italia und Germania* gradually emerged. I hope to show that the work combines in a single image a multitude of meanings and allusions, of which the title evokes only one, and that it is in fact an unusually effective icon of the general Romantic aspiration – fervently espoused in the circle of Friedrich Schlegel, with which Overbeck was closely associated during the Schlegels' residence in Rome – to transgress boundaries and reconcile or reunite seeming opposites, such as female and male, poetry and philosophy, art and religion, imagination and truth, the venerated past and the "splendid and beautiful" present, without repudiating either term. In Overbeck's own words, these seeming opposites should rather be thought of "as joined in a beautiful and deeply felt friendship . . . not separate and exclusive of each other but . . . united in harmony and mutual respect." If Caspar David Friedrich's *Der Wanderer über dem Nebelmeer* [*The Wayfarer over the Sea of Mist*] **(Fig. II)** can be viewed as having given iconic expression to the Romantic (perhaps especially Protestant) sense of courageous loneliness in the sublime immensity of nature, Overbeck's *Italia und Germania* may be considered an icon of the Romantic (perhaps especially Catholic) longing to rediscover an earlier ideal of love, reconciliation, and communion. This ideal receives visual expression

[6]In a 1928 catalogue intended to bring the Nazarene painters back into public view and esteem in Germany (*Die Malerei der deutschen Romantiker und Nazarener im besonderen Overbecks und seines Kreises* [Munich: Kurt Wolff Verlag]) the art historian and curator Kurt Karl Eberlein explicitly offers *Sulamith und Maria* as an alternative title for *Italia und Germania* (Plate 13).

[7]Howitt, I:386-87.

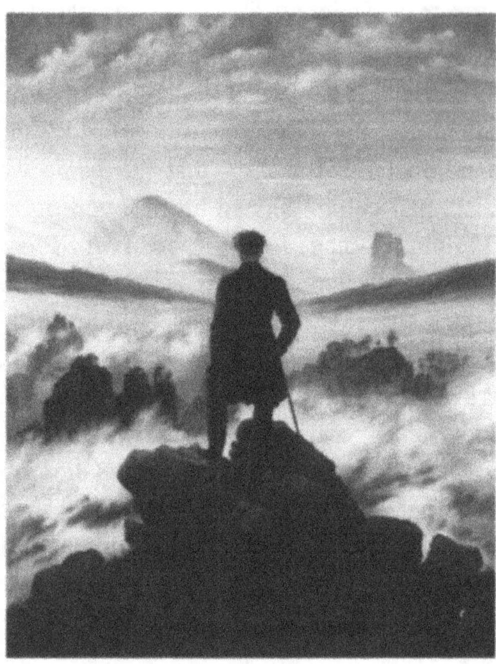

Fig. II. Caspar David Friedrich. *Der Wanderer über dem Nebelmeer.* (circa1818). Oil on canvas. 74.8 × 94.8 cm. Hamburg, Kunsthalle. http://commons.wikimedia.org/wiki/Image:Caspar_David_Friedrich_032.jpg (The Yorck Project/GFDL)

through the beautiful oval formed within the painting's classic pyramidal composition by the arms, necklines, and heads of the two figures and through the color relations, which simultaneously individualize the figures (the red of the left-hand figure's bodice contrasting with the green of the right-hand figure's) and unite them (the red of the left-hand figure being picked up in the full skirt of the right-hand figure and the green of the right-hand figure being reiterated in the left-hand figure's crown of laurel leaves). Instead of the scene of tumultuous, luminous, and sublime nature that dominates Friedrich's painting and on which the standing figure of the somberly clad, lone male wayfarer, his back turned to the viewer, looks out (along with the viewer himself), Overbeck's brightly and distinctly colored canvas is almost entirely filled by the handsomely attired, hand-clasping, seated female couple, whom the artist has placed in the foreground in three-quarter view or in profile, with, as background, a reassuring human landscape of churches and houses. Where Friedrich's painting presents the viewer with the dramatic spectacle of man – contemporary man, in contemporary dress – directly facing the power of divine, untamed nature, Overbeck's painting connects its monumentally conceived human figures not only with each other but with history, culture, and tradition. The divine is here represented not by nature, which is relegated to the far distance and depicted as picturesque rather than sublime, but by ecclesiastical architecture (Romanesque and Italianate behind Italia, Gothic and Northern behind Germania); the two figures are dressed in rich Renaissance costume; and the painting itself refers to an earlier artistic tradition with which, across an interval of misdirection, it deliberately aims to re-establish continuity.

The earliest versions of what later became *Italia und Germania* were Overbeck's contribution to a series of closely related images produced by him and his intimate friend and fellow-artist Franz Pforr. As students at the Vienna Art Academy in the first decade of the nineteenth century the eighteen-year-old Overbeck and the nineteen-year-old Pforr had formed one of those intense friendships for which Germans of the neoclassical and Romantic periods seem to have had a special talent.[8] Overbeck was the youngest son of a lawyer, senator, diplomat, and fairly popular poet (two delightful little poems by him were set to music by Mozart) from the ancient Hanseatic free city of Lübeck, of which toward the end of his life he became Bürgermeister. I will have more to say later about this attractive figure, who could easily have served as a model for "old Johann Buddenbrook," the kindly, witty, free-spirited grandfather in Thomas Mann's great family novel *Buddenbrooks*. (Mann was also, of course, a native of Lübeck.) Young Johann Friedrich – or Fritz, as he was called in his own family circle – gave early signs of artistic talent and his father arranged for him to take lessons with a painter friend, Nikolaus Peroux. In 1806, on the advice of various other artist friends, Christian Adolf Overbeck had his son enrolled in the Vienna Academy, which was then, under its director, Heinrich Füger, one of the most highly regarded in Germany.

Franz Pforr was the son of a fairly well known animal painter, Johann Georg Pforr, and the nephew, on his mother's side, of another animal and landscape artist, Johann Heinrich Tischbein the Younger (1742-1808), and of the latter's better-known brother, "Goethe-Tischbein" (1751-1829), the friend

[8]Overbeck wrote to his father on 19.12.1807 that he felt he had reached a turning point in his life, "da ich den Werth eines Freundes, eines gleichgesinnten Herzens habe kennen gelernt, dem man sich ganz anvertrauen kann, in dem man sich selbst wiederfindet, und der das ungeschränkteste Vertrauen und die aufrichtigste Liebe mit der innigsten Freundschaft und der zuvorkommendsten Bereitwilligkeit erwidert. So einen Freund, geliebtester Vater," he went on, "habe ich vor kurzem gewonnen, mit dem ich so wohl an Alter und Neigung, als an Urtheil und Denkungsart und Geschmack so vollkommen übereinstimme, dass wir beyde, wenn wir uns unser Herz eröfffnen und es uns gegenseitig unpartheiisch vorlegen und sowohl von der bessern als von der schlechtern Seit zeigen, einer in dem anderen uns selbst wiederzusehen glaubt." ["I have come to know the value of a friend, of a heart moved in the same way as mine, a being in whom one can have absolute trust, in whom one finds a mirror image of oneself, and who responds to the the most unlimited trust and the most sincere love with the most heartfelt friendship and the most eager desire to be helpful and supportive. I have recently acquired such a friend, dearest father, with whom I am in such harmony with respect not only to age and inclination but to my judgments, my way of thinking, and my tastes, that when we open our hearts to each other and expose honestly what is in them to each other, the bad as well as the good, we both have the impression that we have found ourselves in the other"] (quoted by Frank Büttner, "Bilder als Manifeste der Freundschaft und der Kunstaunschauung zwischen Aufklärung und Romantik in Deutschland," in *Johann Friedrich Overbeck: Italia und Germania*, Catalogue of Exhibition "Italia und Germania," Munich Pinakothek, 20.2 - 14.4.2002; Berlin Alte Nationalgalerie, 13.9 – 15.12.2002 [Munich: Kulturstiftung der Länder und der Staatlichen Graphischen Sammlung München, 2002], p. 19).

and portraitist of Goethe (**Pf. 1**).[9] (The last-named, as it happens, was also an acquaintance of the older Overbeck, who, as a proud father, submitted some of his son's early work to him.[10]) Orphaned early in life, Pforr grew up in Frankfurt in a patrician merchant milieu similar to that of Overbeck in Lübeck. In 1801, at the age of thirteen, he was sent to study with his uncle Johann Heinrich at the Art Academy in Kassel. Four years later he enrolled at the Vienna Academy. Overbeck arrived the following year and by 1807 the two young men had become fast friends – so much so that in 1808, when Overbeck's father, who was in Paris on a diplomatic mission, urged his son to join him in the French capital and take advantage of the outstanding art instruction available there, Overbeck refused. Christian Adolf had guessed that this might happen. "The more I think about it, the more convinced I am that [coming to Paris] is the right move for him to make at this stage of his development," he had written to his wife. "What reason does he have to stay longer in Vienna?" He had also foreseen that "the most serious obstacle will be Pforr, should he not wish to come along," for the two have sworn an oath never to separate, to share good times and bad, and to set out together in two years' time for Italy, on foot, pooling and sharing all their resources.[11]

The uninhibited use of the rhetoric of passionate love in the letters exchanged by Klopstock and Gleim, Fuessli and Lavater, Wackenroder and Tieck, Bonstetten and Johannes Müller or, for that matter, Christian Adolf Overbeck himself and his close friend at Göttingen University, Anton Matthias Sprickmann (later a Professor of Law at Berlin)[12] – to evoke a few friendships among literary men from the late eighteenth and early nineteenth centuries –

[9]**Pf.** followed by arabic numerals refers to images in a digital portfolio viewable at http://www.aps-pub.com/transactions/97_5/. Figures in the printed text are indicated by roman numerals.

[10]Karl Theodor Gaedertz, "Die beiden Overbeck," in his *Was ich am Wege fand: Blätter und Bilder aus Literatur, Kunst und Leben* (Leipzig: Georg Wigand, 1905), p. 79.

[11]*"Beieinanderseyn ist das täglich Brot der Liebe." Briefe C.A. Overbecks an seine Familie aus St. Petersburg 1804 und aus Paris 1807-1811*, Fritz Luchmann, ed. (Lübeck: Schmidt-Römhild, 1992), pp. 220-223, letters of 25.7 and 19.8.1808 (Veröffentlichungen zur Geschichte der Hansestadt Lübeck, Reihe B, Band 21). Their son had drawn up a list of reasons for staying in Vienna, Overbeck Senior wrote his wife from Paris: "Nature, he says, is his academy, and this academy is as available to him there [in Vienna] as here [in Paris] . . . Classical models . . . are adequately represented there and ready to hand, and good engravings can be had of things from Paris. . . . It is as easy to earn money there, he claims, as here (to the extent that it is possible to consider that at all). . . . Living expenses are no higher there than here, perhaps lower. . . . As for being safe – there is as little danger of military service there as here. And lastly a young man should not be too sure of himself. The greater the attractions, the easier it is to be seduced." But the essential reason for not leaving Vienna, Overbeck Senior wrote, was the friendship with Pforr. The various, more or less plausible arguments, "all rest *in fine finali* on the principal point (which I have to say I find a little strange), namely the friendship with Pforr." While Overbeck Senior had the highest regard for his son's talents and goodness of heart, and never attempted to force him into adopting any line of action, in the planned communal life with Pforr, he noted, "it is easy to see which of the two [the heart or the head], has the gift of the gab. Everyone knows the heart is a formidable Sophist."

[12]See Heinz Jansen, ed., *Aus dem Göttinger Hainbund: Overbeck und Sprickmann* (Münster i. Westf.: Regenbergsche Verlagsbuchhandlung, 1933), especially pp. 169-70, letter from Overbeck to Sprickmann, 29.5.1781. As students at Göttingen, Overbeck and Sprickmann had both been closely associated with former members of the Göttingen Hainbund, a circle of poets, all admirers of Klopstock, formed at the University in 1772.

should not mislead us into thinking of these *Sturm und Drang* and early Romantic relationships as contrived, purely sentimental or, from our modern perspective, homoerotic, even though there was probably a good deal of sentiment, and possibly some tincture of homoeroticism, in them. In Germany, it has been said, with its numerous small and confining "feudal-absolutist" states, friendship at the end of the eighteenth century was "the concrete embodiment of a utopian community in which the individual would be able to develop to the full both socially and emotionally." Offering the possibility of socialization in conditions of freedom and equality, friendship represented the realization, on the modest scale of private, interpersonal relations, of the utopian dream of reforming the social order of the decrepit *ancien régime* from the inside out.[13] Sometimes it extended beyond two persons to embrace several, who might choose to bind themselves together by the swearing of an oath, in a more or less formal *Bund* or league.[14] As the political dimension of the friendship leagues prior to the notorious student *Burschenschaften* was not usually well defined beyond a rather effusive German patriotism and desire for social improvement, there was often room, especially among individuals close to the Pietist movement, for a significant religious strain in them. According to one historian, the *Bund* or association of friends raised expectations of salvation, whether of a small conventicle, of the nation, or of all humanity.[15] In addition, though God, and more particularly Christ, was the Friend par excellence, the individual's love of Christ readily found concrete expression in a human friend, viewed as an incarnation of the longed for divine presence. In his epic poem *Messias*, Friedrich Gottlieb Klopstock (1724-1803), a poet much influenced by Pietism and much loved in the Overbeck household – as a young man, Overbeck Senior described a journey he made to Hamburg to visit him in terms befitting a pilgrimage to the shrine of a saint[16] – evoked in passionate language the divine bond of friendship uniting Eloa and Gabriel (*Messias,* I, 312-328), Abdiel and Abbadona (*Messias*, II, 627-658), John and Jesus (*Messias*, III, 479-93). "L'image qui s'impose avant tout," observes a French scholar, "c'est

[13]Eckhardt Meyer-Krentler, *Der Bürger als Freund* (Munich: Wilhelm Fink Verlag, 1984), quoted by Frank Büttner, "Bilder als Manifeste der Freundschaft und der Kunstaunschauung zwischen Aufklärung und Romantik in Deutschland," in *Johann Friedrich Overbeck: Italia und Germania* (as in note 8), p. 15. As a utopian social model friendship was superior to love between the sexes; hence Overbeck's notation in his diary, shortly before the death of Pforr in 1812, at the age of 24: "Pforr! Mein Bruder! Deine Liebe war mir sonderlicher als Frauenliebe" ["Pforr! My brother! Your love was dearer to me than the love of women"]. (Cit. Howitt, I: 207)

[14]In some ways these *Bünde* were a less inclusive, more focused, masculine version of the salons of the same period that were hosted by intelligent and cultivated – often Jewish – women, such as Henriette Herz in Berlin and Fanny von Arnstein in Vienna. The salons have been viewed by modern historians as utopian spaces allowing for the formation and cultivation of social and intellectual relationships that would not have been possible in the strictly stratified world outside them.

[15]Reinhard Koselleck, "Bund (Bündnis, Föderalismus, Bundesstaat)" in *Geschichtliche Grundbegriffe*, 1 (Stuttgart, E. Klett, 1972), p. 640.

[16]Heinz Jansen, ed., *Aus dem Göttinger Hainbund: Overbeck und Sprickmann* (as in note 12), p. 69. See also Sprickmann's account of visiting Klopstock, ibid., pp. 65-66.

celle de Jean appuyant tendrement sa tête sur la poitrine de Jésus, c'est l'image du couple." "Gehört denn die Freundschaft, gehört unsere Freundschaft," Klopstock himself wrote in a letter to the poet Gleim (31 July 1752), "zu den weltlichen Dingen?"[17] ["Does friendship, does our friendship belong among the things of this world?"] Friendship, as practiced in certain milieux in Germany around the turn of the eighteenth and nineteenth centuries, thus often implied not only a desire for social and political change but a religious aspiration toward transformation, redemption, and union with the divine.[18]

Within a year of their first meeting Overbeck and Pforr had discovered that, despite some differences in taste (Overbeck was more drawn to religious subjects and to the early Italian painters, Pforr to subjects from national history and legend and to the Old German school), they shared a common critical view not only of the traditional instruction they were receiving at the Academy (this required years of copying from old masters in all styles before the student got to undertake any original work of his own) but of the content and objectives of that instruction and of the eclecticism to which, in their view, it led. Essentially, the two young men had come, in the course of many conversations about art, to reject the baroque and rococo tradition with its emphasis on painterly technique, illusionist effects, and sensuous visual pleasure and to demand that art become, once again, what they claimed it had been in its greatest days: a vehicle for the expression and communication of spiritual truths and inner spiritual experiences. In this regard their position, with respect to the plastic arts, was not unlike that of Klopstock with respect to poetry.[19] Increasingly, they looked for inspiration to the more severe art of the early German and Italian schools, to Dürer, Perugino, and the young Raphael. Describing a visit that the two of them paid to the reopened Imperial art collection in the Belvedere Palace, Pforr relates that both found their judgment of earlier works of art had undergone a revolution.

> As we entered, I can almost say that we were stunned. Everything now looked different to us. We hurried past a large number of paintings, to which we had previously been attracted, with a feeling of dissatisfaction. Other works, in contrast, which had formerly left us cold, now drew us irresistibly. . . . Paintings by Tintoretto, Veronese, Maratti, even some by the Carracci, Correggio, Guido, and Titian that we had once looked on with amazement, now made a feeble impression on us. It often seemed to us that a cold heart lay behind bold brushstrokes and striking color effects or that the highest goal the painter had set

---

[17]Jean Murat, *F.G. Klopstock: les thèmes principaux de son oeuvre* (Paris: Les Belles Lettres, 1959), p. 184. (Publications de la Faculté des Lettres de l'Université de Strasbourg, 138). Letter to Gleim, cited, ibid.

[18]See Bertha Baumgärtel, *Angelika Kauffmann (1741-1807). Bedingungen weiblicher Kreativität in der Malerei des 18. Jahrhunderts* (Weinheim/Basel: Beltz, 1990), pp. 186-87 *et passim*.

[19]Murat (as in note 17), pp. 329-36.

himself was no more than the stimulation of a voluptuous sensibility. In contrast, we could hardly tear ourselves away from a St. Justina by Pordenone, some works by Michelangelo and Perugino and a painting from the school of Raphael. . . . The painters of the Dutch school seemed to us to have often sought out excessively unworthy subjects or to have presented nobler ones in an excessively vulgar manner. What we once took to be nature in them, now seemed like caricature. As we hurried from there to the German school, how pleasantly surprised we were; with what purity and charm the latter spoke to us! Much here had once struck us as stiff and forced, but now we had to recognize that our judgment had been distorted by constant contemplation of paintings in which every artistic technique, however ordinary, has been exaggerated, often to the point of ridiculous affectation, and that, as a result, we had taken gestures drawn from nature as she truly is to be stiff and lacking in appropriate movement. Their noble simplicity ["*edle Einfalt*" – almost certainly an allusion to the qualities of "*edle Einfalt und stille Grösse*," noble simplicity and serene grandeur, attributed to ancient Greek art by the champion of a return to the art of Antiquity in the mid-eighteenth century, Johann Joachim Winckelmann] . . . spoke directly to our hearts.[20]

Painting had begun to decline, the two friends now believed, as its earlier close connection with religion was loosened and it began, often still by way of traditional religious topoi, to serve and celebrate worldly rather than spiritual values – prestige, power, and the pleasures of the material universe; that is, as it turned from the communication, by visual means, of spiritual truths, to the

[20]"Bei unserem Eintritt kann ich fast sagen erschracken wir: alles zeigte sich uns anders, an einer Menge von Bildern eilten wir unbefriedigt hinweg, die uns vorher angezogen hatten, und andere hingegen, die uns ehemals kalt gelassen hatten, rissen uns nun unwiderstehlich hin. Keiner wagte dem andern seine Gedanken mitzutheilen, weil jeder fürchtete, eine gewisse Eitelkeit leitete sein Urtheil; endlich eröffneten wir uns, und wie überraschend war es, dass einer wie der andere dachte! Bilder von Tintoret, Paul Veronese, Maratti, ja selbst welche von den Caraccis, von Coreggio, Guido und Titian, die wir sonst angestaunt hatten, machten nur eine sehr schwache Wirkung noch, wir sahen oft ein kaltes Herz hinter kühnen Pinzelzügen und schönen Farben verborgen, oder dass der Maler zum höchsten Ziel sich nur die Erweckung einer sinnlichen wohllüstigen Empfindung genommen hatte. Hingegen konnten wir uns kaum losreissen von einer heiligen Justina von Pordenone, von ein paar Bilder von Michel Angelo, Perugino und einem aus der Schule von Raphael. Mit Freude sahen wir bei ihnen bestätigt, was uns unser Innerstes über die Behandlung der Kunst sagte. Die Maler der niederländischen Schule schienen uns ihre Gegenstände oft zu unwürdig ausgesucht, oder die erhabeneren zu niedrig vorgestellt zu haben; was sonst uns Natur bei ihnen dünkte, schien uns jetzt oft Karikatur. Wir eilten in die deutsche Schule, wie angenehm überraschte sie uns, wie lieblich und rein sprach hier jede Empfindung uns an. Manches schien uns sonst hier steif und gezwungen, jetzt mussten wir gestehen, dass das beständige Betrachten von Gemälden, welche eine jede Berrichtung, wenn sie auch noch so gewöhnlich ist, in einer übertriebenen oft bis zum Lächerlichen affektirten Stellung zeigten, unser Urtheil irre geführt hatte, und dass wir desswegen diese aus der wirklichen Natur aufgefassten Gebärden für steif und ohne die gehörige Bewegung geachtet hatten. Die edle Einfalt sprach mit der bestimmten Charakteristik laut an unser Herz, hier war keine Bravur des Pinsels, keine kühne Behandlungsart, enfach stand alles da, als wäre es nicht gemalt sondern so gewachsen" (quoted in Howitt, 1:82-83). Pforr's early negative judgment of the Venetians was repeated by Overbeck in the explanatory text he wrote several decades later for his monumental "Triumph of Religion in the Arts" (Staedel Museum, Frankfurt am Main): "The Venetians went astray as soon as they made colouring the principal object of attraction, and so by degrees they sank in sensuality" (quoted in J. Beavington Atkinson, *Overbeck* [London: Samspon Low; New York: Scribner and Welford, 1882], p. 68).

representation of reality as empirically experienced by the senses, albeit often in a heightened or embellished form. With the Venetians the technical side of painting had been developed with great brilliance as the medium of such representation, they claimed, and art had entered on a path of decadence, which it was still following (a view later developed by many early Romantics, including the philosopher Friedrich Schlegel and the early art historian Friedrich von Rumohr), and from which the two young students felt it was their mission to rescue it. To Franz Pforr the painter's brushstrokes were only "a necessary evil, no more than a means to an end," and he considered it "nonsense to praise an artist's audacity in this area or find something to brag about in it."[21]

Together with four other students at the Academy, who sympathized with their goals, Overbeck and Pforr banded together in 1808 in an association or *Bund*, to which they gave the name of the patron saint of painting. The goal to which the members of the *Lukasbund* or Brotherhood of St. Luke pledged on oath to dedicate themselves was nothing less than the radical reform of art through restoration of the lost unity of art and religion and thereby, they claimed, of the former close relation between art and the people. Art, the young *Lukasbrüder* held, was not about technique and not about providing a privileged few with sensuous pleasures; it should not be content to be, as Peter Cornelius, who joined Overbeck and Pforr a few years later, was to put it, "eine feile Dienerin üppiger Grossen, eine Krämerin, und niedrige Modezofe" ["an easy-going serving maid, ready to sell herself to the rich and powerful, a shopkeeper hawking her wares, a common salesgirl of the latest fashions"].[22] Works of art should not be objects that wealthy private persons buy, sell, and invest in. In

---

[21]Hebert Lehr, *Die Blütezeit romantischer Bildkunst: Franz Pforr der Meister des Lukasbundes* (Marburg an der Lahn: Verlag des kunstgeschichtlichen Seminars, 1924), p. 38; Sabine Fastert, *Die Entdeckung des Mittelalters. Geschichtsrezeption in der nazarenischen Malerei des frühen 19. Jahrhunderts* (Munich and Berlin: Deutscher Kunstverlag, 2000) p. 56. Anton Friedrich Justus Thibaut's *Reinheit der Tonkunst* (Heidelberg: J.C.B. Mohr, 1825), a work that impressed the young Felix Mendelssohn, seems to have staked out a similar position in music. According to one modern scholar, "Palestrina was [Thibaut's] god. . . . He was also enamoured of Orlando di Lasso." Mozart, in contrast, had spoiled Handel's *Messiah* with his "dubious instrumentation." While he did useful research on music in Rome and Vienna and had dug up many old manuscripts, Thibaut, we are told, "was completely unaware of all the developments that had taken place in the orchestra since the late Baroque period. This arch-conservative was horrified by the 'vainglory of the instruments, their impulse to exceed themselves.' " Modern musicological scholarship makes the same judgment of Thibaut as modern art history has made of the Nazarenes. "As we know today, his book did enormous harm; perhaps only a non-musician could have written so wrong-headed a work" (Heinrich Eduard Jacob, *Felix Mendelssohn and His Times*, trans. Richard and Clara Winston [London: Barrie, 1963], pp. 72-73).

[22]Quoted by Büttner (as in note 8), p. 21. In a letter of 3.11.1814 to Joseph Görres, then editor of the *Rheinischer Merkur*, Cornelius outlined the Nazarenes' aspirations for an art that would once again fill the people's life with beauty, like that of the Middle Ages, and speak to it in colorful and effective language "from the walls of our high cathedrals, our quiet chapels and lonely monasteries, from our town halls and merchants' warehouses" ["von den Wänden der hohen Dome, der stillen Kapellen und einsamen Klöster, den Raths- und Kaufhäusern und Hallen herab"] restoring to a new generation "the old faith, the old love, and, along with them, the old strength of our fathers" and thus "reconciling the Lord our God with His people" ["dass der alte Glaube, die alte Liebe, und mit ihnen die alte Kraft der Väter wieder erwacht sei, und darum der Herr unser Gott wieder ausgesöhnt sey mit seinem Volke"] (Joseph v. Görres, *Gesammelte Schriften*, Marie Görres, ed., 9 vols. [Munich: In Commission der literarisch-artistischen Anstalt, 1854–1874], 8:439).

order to thrive and prosper, art had to be an expression of spirituality, it had to be the vehicle through which the highest and purest truths – truths that are the essential concern of an entire people, indeed of all human beings – are communicated to all by visual means. It is not surprising that the *Lukasbrüder* were soon to be attracted by large-scale fresco painting as a medium more appropriate to the function they attributed to art than the easily transportable canvases of the easel-painter in oil, that they laid almost as much store by the cartoons for their paintings as by the paintings themselves, or that Peter Cornelius could denounce the brush for having "become the ruin of art" and for having led art "from Nature to Mannerism."[23] Appropriately, the motto of the *Lukasbund* was "*Wahrheit*" – truth – but that word in no way meant the realistic rendering of objects, people, or scenes in the empirically experienced world.

To achieve the desired revolution in art, moreover, it was not sufficient to make technical adjustments. In order to recognize the higher truths that it was his task to represent to the community, the artist himself had to have a pure heart and to be motivated by the highest ideals. Overbeck's own father, the devoted admirer of Klopstock, had made that point in a letter he wrote to his son at the time of the latter's departure for Vienna in 1806. "Hold on to your religious expression in your art," he advised. "I have noticed with pleasure that it comes naturally to you. If your heart is a temple, only holy figures and divine images will be found there and that noble, heavenly element will shimmer through even representations of the profane world. Then you will have achieved that which raises art to the highest peak: your brush will breathe ennobling notes by which mankind is improved, for one always comes away improved from every master work of heavenly genius."[24] A similar emphasis on the

---

[23]"Der Pinsel ist der Verderb unserer Kunst geworden, er führte von der Natur ab zum Manierismus" (quoted by Richard Muther, *Geschichte der Malerei im XIX Jahrhundert*, 3 vols. [Munich: G. Hirth's Kunstverlag, 1893], vol. 1, p. 218; Engl. trans. *The History of Modern Painting*, 4 vols. [London: J.M. Dent; New York: E.P. Dutton, 1907], vol 1, p. 151). Late-nineteenth-century German art historians, with few exceptions, were sympathetic to Realism and Impressionism and unenthusiastic about Cornelius's attitude to paint and brushwork. Wölfflin, for instance, pointed with satisfaction to the fact that later German painters, including the "Deutsch-Römer" (Feuerbach, Böcklin, Marées), learned from the French and the Belgians to take a different approach to paint. Wölfflin quotes Feuerbach: "I can never thank the master [Thomas Couture] enough for having steered me away from the German obsession with painstaking, invisible brushwork toward a loose handling of impasto and from strict adherence to academic formulas toward bold conception and design" (reported in Heinrich Wölfflin, *Kunstgeschichte des 19. Jahrhunderts. Akademische Vorlesung*, [given at Berlin in 1911] Norbert Schautz, ed. [Alfter: VDG Verlag und Datenbank für Geisteswissenschaftern, 1993], p. 10). In the aftermath of the First World War, however, a new generation of German artists again became critical of "Tafelmalerei" ["easel painting"] as a form of art appropriate to bourgeois egoism and dreamed, like the Nazarenes, of a return to public art in the form of "Wandmalerei" ["mural painting"]. According to the left-wing Cologne artist F.W. Seiwert in 1923, easel painting, "the rise of which coincides not accidentally but out of inner necessity with the rise of modern capitalism . . . has become impossible" (quoted by Peter Hielscher, "Georg Grosz in der Turnhalle: zum politischen Wandbild in der Weimarer Republik," in *Wem gehört die Welt: Kunst und Gesellschaft in der Weimarer Republik*, Exhibition Catalogue [Berlin, 1977], pp. 268-79, at p. 275). "Wandmalerei" was also the dream of Heinrich Vogeler, the Jugendstil artist turned Communist. Not surprisingly, one of the visitors to Vogeler's estate in Worpswede, which he had turned into a commune and a home for the children of executed or imprisoned left-wing activists and where he himself had executed murals (later destroyed by the Nazis) was the Mexican muralist Diego Rivera.

[24]Quoted in Gaedertz (as in note 10), p. 78. See also J. Beavington Atkinson, *Overbeck* (as in note 20), p. 8.

artist's inner spiritual condition is expressed in some verses by a young friend and collaborator of Overbeck's, who was inducted into the *Lukasbund* in 1815 – the Jewish-born painter Philipp Veit, a son of Dorothea Schlegel's and, like his mother, a convert to Christianity:

> Was hilft mir Kunst und Wissenschaft,
> Wenn diese Kunst ich nimmer lerne,
> Wie durch der heil'gen Liebe Kraft
> Ich von mir selbst mich selbst entferne,
> Gereinigt schon auf dieser Erde,
> Zum sanften Kinde wieder werde.[25]

["Of what use to me are art and science as long as I fail to learn the essential art of distancing myself from myself through the power of holy love and, already purified on this earth, becoming once again a gentle child."]

The transformation of art required, in other words, the inner conversion of the artist. It is no accident that, as we shall see shortly, religious conversion was a frequent occurrence among the Nazarene artists, as the later followers of Overbeck and Pforr were dubbed (as much for their way of wearing their hair – long to the shoulders and parted down the middle – as for their overt piety),[26] or that the Lukas brothers' model of an artistic community was essentially monastic.

The *Lukasbund*'s revolt against the baroque and rococo was not an isolated phenomenon. An earlier critique of the baroque and rococo had been initiated around the middle of the eighteenth century in the name of a return to the original models of ancient art. Exactly five years after a celebrated Swiss Jean-Jacques produced a prize essay attacking what he alleged was a decadent culture in the name of nature, Johann Joachim Winckelmann, launched a radical critique of contemporary art and sculpture and called for a return to the pure sources of the antique in ancient Greece. Characteristically, Winckelmann's chief interest was sculpture, rather than painting. He was unconcerned by, perhaps insensitive to the specifically painterly qualities of color, tone, and chiaroscuro, and in his comments on painting, he judged line and composition – that is to say the most ideal, abstract, and essentialist elements of painting – to be far more important than color, light, or illusionist effect. As Winckelmann's neo-classicism came later to be seen as standing in opposition to the return to Christian art being

[25]"Liebessehnen," from *Oelzweige*, G. Passy and J. P. Silbert, eds. (Vienna: Geistliche Leihbibliothek, 1819–1823), 2:116, quoted in *Dorothea von Schlegel geb. Mendelssohn und deren Söhne Johannes und Philipp Veit: Briefwechsel*, J.M. Reich, ed. (Mainz: Franz Kirchheim, 1881), 2 vols., 2:454. Cf. a comment by the painter Louise Seidler: "In der Tat malt man nur gut, wenn man aus dem Innersten des Gemüthes herausmalt." ["It is indeed the case that one only paints well when one paints from the innermost core of one's being."] (*Erinnerungen und Leben der Malerin Louise Seidler [geboren zu Jena 1786, gestorben zu Weimar 1866]*, Hermann Uhde, ed. [Berlin: Wilhelm Hertz, 1874], p. 242).

[26]On the naming of the Nazarenes or "Nazarites," see Atkinson, *Overbeck* (as in note 20), p. 25, and Keith Andrews, *The Nazarenes: A Brotherhood of German Painters* (Oxford: Clarendon Press, 1964), p. 29.

advocated by the *Lukasbrüder* and those who gathered around them, it is worth emphasizing not only that the *Lukasbrüder* borrowed, consciously or unconsciously, the vocabulary of Winckelmann,[27] but that the champion of German neoclassicism expressed opinions about the relation of line, color, and painterly technique that clearly anticipate those of the deeply religious, Christian, and anticlassical Nazarenes several decades later.

As early as his *Gedanken über die Nachahmung der griechischen Werke in der Malerei und Bildhauerkunst* of 1755 Winckelmann repeatedly evoked the "Ruhe und Stille" of Raphael in contrast to the work of later painters like Caravaggio and the Dutch. To many people these qualities – repose and stillness – may seem lifeless ["leblos"], he acknowledged, anticipating the criticism that would be leveled later at the Nazarenes, but to the practiced eye they are noble and meaningful ["bedeutend und erhaben"]. Winckelmann singled out the Dresden *Madonna* of Raphael for special praise: "Look at the Madonna, with her face full of innocence and her more than merely feminine grandeur, in a posture of blessed calm, characterized by that tranquillity that the Ancients imparted to their divinities. How grand and noble her entire contour is."[28] A few years later in his celebrated *Geschichte der Kunst des Altertums* (1764) [*History of the Art of Antiquity*] Winckelmann noted how some late classical writers had found fault with the sculptor Myron because of what they described as the "hardness" of his manner. This showed, according to Winckelmann, that "the ancient writers very often judged of art in the same manner as the moderns; for the firmness of drawing, the correctness and severity of Raphael's figures have appeared hard and stiff to many when compared with the softness of the outlines and the round and suavely treated forms of Correggio." In truth, however, Winckelmann maintained, once again anticipating both the technical preferences of the Nazarenes and the criticism later art historians and some contemporaries would make of their work, "just as in learning music and speech it is necessary to produce the tones of the former and the syllables of the latter with sharp clarity in order to achieve purity, harmony, and beauty of expression, so drawing leads to truth and beauty of form in art not through vague, fluid, suggestive pen- or brushstrokes, but through manly and exactly defined outlines, even if these are somewhat hard."[29] Aptly enough, Overbeck's father once

[27]Pforr's reference to "edle Einfalt" has already been noted. In 1811 Johannes Veit referred in similar vein to the "stille Grösse" of the Sistine Chapel, *Dorothea von Schlegel geb. Mendelssohn und deren Söhne: Briefwechsel* (as in note 25), 2:28-29.

[28]Quoted from J.J. Winckelmann, *Ewiges Griechentum: Auswahl aus seinen Schriften und Briefen*, Fritz Forschepiepe, ed. (Munich: Kröner Verlag, 1943), pp. 15-16, 23-25.

[29]J.J. Winckelmann, *Geschichte der Kunst des Altertums* (Vienna: Phaidon Verlag, 1934 [orig. 1764], 216-18), quoted from the English trans. by G. Henry Lodge, *The History of Ancient Art*, 4 vols. (Boston: James R. Osgood, 1872), 3:199-200. Likewise, 3:176: "The patriarchs of modern art, even in its infancy, have done what Raphael did in its greatest bloom: they sketched the outlines of their figures with accuracy and precision, and were not so easily satisfied as are those who are termed *machinists*, that is, those who rapidly execute large works, who sketch their figures in the coarsest manner, and trust for the rest to the good luck of their brush."

expressed the hope that his son might combine "Winckelmann and Raphael in a single individual."[30]

Opposition to the baroque and rococo – which, of course, was by no means confined to Germany but occurred in most Northern European countries as well, to some extent, as in Italy – came from various quarters and took different forms. Its varying motivations sometimes coincided and sometimes entered into conflict with each other. In some cases, as with Winckelmann, it appears to have reflected a passionate commitment to a new aesthetic and humanist ideal. A purified art was seen as offering a model of harmonious, "natural" existence, free of the distortions associated with an irrational social order and a repressive religion or political regime (to Winckelmann, the golden age of classical art was also that of the free, democratic Greek city-state), and as itself the instrument of personal and social transformation. Both Schiller and Goethe gave frequent expression to this point of view. In other cases, opposition to the baroque and rococo was inspired by deeply religious and spiritual aspirations that were felt to be incompatible with esthetic idealism. To the *Lukasbrüder*, the esthetic idealism of the neoclassicists was an illusory and superficial response to the corruption of culture. Help would come only from a return to purity of spirit. Purity of form was not enough.

Patriotic and national feeling was yet another source of opposition to the baroque and the rococo. As the baroque and rococo were generally associated with foreign influences in Germany, notably that of France but also that of the Roman Church, Winckelmann's project of returning to the purity of Greece was viewed by many of its advocates as a means of reinventing a national German culture destroyed by the devastating Thirty Years' War. This patriotic impulse was reinforced when the German lands were again invaded in the early years of the nineteenth century, this time by the armies of Imperial France. The national ideal was also often identified with Protestant Christianity, and more particularly with the Lutheran Evangelical Church, even though major figures in the neoclassical movement, such as Goethe and Schiller, adopted an overtly antireligious stance. (Winckelmann's conversion to Catholicism was widely viewed as opportunistic.) In other words, the national German culture that German artists and writers were striving to create was to be marked, in the eyes of a fair number of writers and artists, by the severe simplicity not only of classical antiquity but of Protestant Reformation Christianity. German neoclassicism was thus to be distinguished from both the worldly, corrupt culture of the baroque and the secular *antiquomanie* of Republican and Imperial France.

This may partly explain the scandal and dismay provoked in 1800 by the sudden conversion to Roman Catholicism of Count Leopold von Stolberg, one

[30]Quoted by Gaedertz (as in note 10), p. 79.

of the leaders of the new classicizing national movement in literature and culture, a highly regarded author of patriotic poems and of translations of Homer and Plato, and a close friend of Johann Heinrich Voss, the author of a translation of the *Iliad* into German that was considered a cornerstone of neoclassicism as the national form of artistic expression. (Both Stolberg and Voss, incidentally, were from Northern Germany and were friends of the Overbeck family.) Voss later publicly accused his erstwhile companion and associate of betraying by his conversion the national cause to which both had been committed. Stolberg, however, like the strongly Pietist-influenced Klopstock, had had a deeply religious conception of art, not unlike that of the *Lukasbrüder*, from the beginning. As early as 1788 he was arguing that art must serve religion and truth ("Wahrheit") or remain arid and merely decorative.[31] Even before his conversion, he had publicly criticized Schiller's alleged estheticism and this had led to an estrangement from Goethe, with whom Stolberg and his brother had previously enjoyed cordial relations. As for the national, patriotic movement, as it grew increasingly xenophobic in the last years of the struggle against the French and in the years following the Congress of Vienna, both the neohumanists and some of the partisans of a new religious art distanced themselves from it,[32] without, however, making common cause. Although both looked back for inspiration to pre-baroque models and while their esthetic tastes were in important respects not far apart, their understanding and expectations of art were different.

[31]According to Stolberg, "Auch die Poesie kommt von Gott! dürfen wir kühn sagen; aber nur ihr wahrer Gebrauch heiliget sie. Ihre Bestimmung ist Wahrheit zu zeigen . . . Poesie, welche nicht der Wahrheit gewidmet ist, schimmert ohne zu wärmen." ["We may boldly affirm that poetry too comes from God. But only through its true use is it sanctified. Its proper purpose is to show Truth. Poetry that does not serve Truth glistens but does not warm."] (Quoted in *"Wohne immer in meinem Herzen und in den Herzen meiner Freunde allesbelebende Liebe!" Friedrich Leopold Graf zu Stolberg [1750-1819]*, Ellmar Mittler and Inka Tappenbeck, eds. [Göttingen Niedersächsische Staats- und Universitätsbibliothek, 2001], p. 78; see also Ludwig Stockinger, "Friedrich Leopold Stolbergs Konversion als 'Zeitzeugnis'," in *Friedrich Leopold Graf zu Stolberg [1750-1819]. Beiträge zum Eutiner Symposium im September 1997*, Frank Bandach, Jürgen Behrens, Ute Pott, eds. [Eutin: Struve's Buchdruckerei und Verlag, 2002], pp. 217-18.)

[32]Thus Stolberg wrote to his brother in 1815 of ever louder "ranting" ["Poltern"] about "a so-called German-ness ['einem sogenannten Deutschtum'] and of such despicable contempt for everything foreign that one might easily become fearful of what could happen if this spirit were to spread and become predominant. "The patriot of earlier years now warned against an "egoistischer Patriotismus" and the blind idolatry of Teutonism ["Abgötterey der Teutschheit"]. These, he says, "are in contradiction with our true character" (quoted in Dirk Hempel, *Friedrich Leopold Graf zu Stolberg (1750-1819): Staatsmann und politischer Schriftsteller* [Weimar/Cologne,Vienna: Böhlau, 1997], p. 242). Henriette Mendelssohn, Dorothea Schlegel's sister, who underwent a sincere conversion in 1814, had begun, as early as 1812, to question the fanatical patriotism of the period of the War of Liberation. While she admires Friedrich Schlegel's zeal, she writes to Dorothea, "it seems to me that patriotism cannot truly be a Christian virtue and that hatred of other nations is incompatible with the charity that Christ preached and enjoined us to practice. If everyone makes an effort to be a human being and a Christian, we will no longer have need of the loose bond of love for our own nation. . . . Our Lord suffered for all humanity, not for this or that nation" (*Dorothea Schlegel, geb. Mendelssohn und deren Söhne Johannes und Philipp Veit: Briefwechsel* [as in note 25], 2: 110). As for Overbeck, as late as 1865, with nationalist sentiment growing ever stronger in Germany, he affirmed that he was a Christian first and only "demnach Deutscher" ["a German second"]. Without wishing to make light of his affection for his homeland, he explained, he believed that the "heavenly fatherland" was "incomparably higher" than the earthly one (Howitt, 2:385). Overbeck's decision to spend his entire life in Rome rather than return to Germany conveys unmistakably where his primary allegiance lay.

Nevertheless, it is doubtful that the *Lukasbrüder* could have formulated their own goals without the precedent of neoclassicism. The *Lukasbrüder* in particular and the Nazarenes in general certainly turned against neoclassical themes and the neoclassical ideal, seeing them as elitist, illusory, and alien to the German popular tradition. A fair number of them also came – like Stolberg – to see Protestantism as deeply involved in many of the aspects of modernity that they rejected[33] and they renounced it in favor of a return to the Roman Church. Still, as noted, they also shared some essential artistic values with Winckelmann and borrowed his language at times. On their arrival in Rome, moreover, they quickly won the support of several important neoclassical artists, such as the sculptors Bertel Thorvaldsen and Antonio Canova, the Tyrolese painter Anton Koch, and the Württemberg painter and student of David, Gottlieb Schick, much admired for his *Apollo among the Shepherds* **(Pf. 2)** – one of the most explicit statements of the neohumanist ideal[34] – as well as for his portraits of the wife and children of Wilhelm von Humboldt, a leading figure in the neohumanist movement. Schick's work was also much appreciated in the circle of Friedrich Schlegel. Yet both Humboldt's wife, Caroline, and Friedrich Schlegel (who converted to Catholicism with his Jewish wife, Dorothea, originally Brendel Mendelssohn, the daughter of the admired Enlightenment philosopher and friend of Lessing, Moses Mendelssohn) were also major champions of the *Lukasbrüder* and of the Nazarene movement in general. A painting by Wilhelm von Schadow, one of two artist sons of the prominent neoclassical Berlin sculptor Gottfried Schadow, and a close friend of Overbeck's (he was inducted into the *Lukasbund* in 1813 and converted to Catholicism, largely under Overbeck's influence, in 1814), depicts himself, together with his brother, the neoclassical sculptor Ridolfo Schadow, and Thorvaldsen, as three artists committed to the same artistic goals **(Pf. 3, 4)**. In fact, Schick, Koch, Thorvaldsen, and Canova also executed major works on Christian themes **(Pf. 5, 6)**. Despite Goethe's derision, in the name of neoclassicism, of the Nazarenes' "religiös-patriotische Kunst," neoclassical artists and Nazarenes did therefore share significant common ground. In the art historical literature it has mostly been the conflict between the two lines of oppostion to the baroque and rococo that has been highlighted, whereas their connection has tended to be overlooked. A few art historians and at least one respected general historian

[33]Sara Ann Malsch, *The Image of Martin Luther in the Writings of Novalis and Friedrich Schlegel* (Bern: Herbert Lang; Frankfurt/Main: Peter Lange), 1974. On Stolberg's influence on Overbeck, see Brigitte Heise, *Johann Friedrich Overbeck: Das künstlerische Werk und seine literarischen und autobiographischen Quellen* (Cologne/Weimar/Vienna: Böhlau Verlag, 1999), pp. 187-89.

[34]Schick's painting evokes Schiller's *Letters on the Aesthetic Education of Mankind*, in which beauty and art mediate between "form" and "life," order and freedom, the ideal and the real. An earlier watercolor on the same theme by Anton Koch (now in the Nationalgalerie in Berlin) bears the date, inscribed by the artist himself, "1792 im 4. Jahre der Revolution" – a testimonial to the early enthusiasm of many German artists for social, political, and artistic change.

have drawn attention to it, however.[35] The Catholic historian Franz Schnabel even expressed the opinion that the failure of the Nazarene artists to engage durably with the modern world is attributable to their underlying attachment to the deeply conservative artistic values – such as clarity and purity of composition, the primacy of line with respect to color, and the importance of the artist's idea or concept rather than his *pratique* or painterly technique – that were also the values of neoclassicism.[36]

In 1810, when the Vienna Academy was forced to close its doors temporarily to foreigners because of shortages brought on by the war against France, four of the original six members of the *Lukasbund* or brotherhood of St. Luke used the occasion to move from the Austrian capital to Rome, where they hoped to continue their studies in greater freedom than they had enjoyed at the Academy under Füger. After a short stay in the Villa Malta, a favorite haunt of German artists and writers, they found more affordable and more lasting lodgings in the disused convent of San Isidoro, whose Irish monks had been forced out by Napoleon. Here they each had a small cell for sleeping in and another to work in. They shared the chore of cooking their frugal communal meals and gathered together in the refectory in the evening for drawing lessons – at which they took turns modeling for each other. (The only model they actually employed was a young boy called Severio; Overbeck was opposed to the use of female models as likely to arouse impure thoughts.) They also

[35]See in particular Karl Scheffler, *Die europäische Kunst im neunzehnten Jahrhundert: Malerei und Plastik*, 2 vols. (Berlin: Bruno Cassirer Verlag, 1927), vol. 1, pp. 107-108. Scheffler views neoclassical and Nazarene art as alike in that both are "reflective" rather than "naïve," more concerned with theory and ideas than with visual experience and painterly practice, and, as a result, equally trapped in eclecticism, imitation, and mannerism. His negative judgment of both appears to reflect a "modernist" perspective influenced by post-Nietzschean "Lebensphilosophie." This modernist perspective in art might also easly be combined with political and social antimodernism. Julius Langbehn's *Rembrandt als Erzieher* (1890), a classic of antimodernism, anticipates both Scheffler's association of Nazarene art with classicism and his condemnation of it as rationalist, theoretical, and not "organic." A less ideologically charged account of the connection of Nazarene art with neoclassicism can be found in Atkinson, *Overbeck* (as in note 20), pp. 12-13, and especially Neuss, "Das Wesen der Nazarenerkunst und ihre Bedeutung für die deutsche Kunst des 19. Jahrhunderts" (as in note 1).

[36]Franz Schnabel, *Deutsche Geschichte im neunzehnten Jahrhundert*, 2nd ed. (Freiburg i.Br.: Herder, 1951 [1st. ed. 1936]), 4 vols. According to Schnabel, who may have been drawing on both Neuss and Scheffler (see note 35), the Nazarenes "despised the theatricality of the baroque, the frivolity of the rococo, and the soulless rules of [academic] classicism" (4:229). Yet, "inasmuch as classical art aimed to give form to ideas, . . . they still lived within that tradition" (4:231). "It was the painter's task to represent not individual character or sensuously beautiful form but the Typical – measured, inwardly grasped, and relieved of excessively powerful affective expression." Echoing Neuss, Schnabel asserts that "the Nazarenes were not Romantics striving for the infinite in the manner of a Runge or a Caspar David Friedrich; they retained a strong feeling for the objective, the historical, for Church and State as the foundation of the spiritual personality. All these painters continued to think and work along classical lines despite their rejection of the rigid rules of classicism. . . . Thus the Nazarenes, according to their individual style, remained true to the classical ideal of simplicity and clarity of form and carried it over into Christian art. What they created is 'Christian classicism' " (4:232-33). As a result, according to Schnabel, while they were able to revive old forms, they failed to produce "a new and great art," i.e., to realize that dream of a monumental art for their own time that Neuss considered their legacy to modern German art. In a forthcoming article, "Ingres and the Nazarenes: A Historiographical Study," Mitchell Frank traces the perception of an underlying similarity of Nazarene to neoclassical art in the writings of a few progressive art historians and critics, such as Richard Muther and Karl Scheffler, to the rise of formalism in the late nineteenth century.

critiqued each other's work and, in accordance with the seriousness with which they took their artistic vocation, studied literature and philosophy together and gave talks to each other on topics of art and aesthetics. One can think of them as a kind of New School or free academy, at which, in contrast to the ancien régime that they had left behind at the Vienna Academy, all participated on an equal footing, learned from each other, were simultaneously masters and pupils, and were free to seek their own way of carrying out the general policy of the brotherhood instead of being obliged to follow specific models.[37] Overbeck himself referred to the group as a *Künstlerrepublik*,[38] whereas Ferdinand Olivier, another young artist from Vienna who was invited to join the Brotherhood in Rome in 1817, noted in his letter of acceptance that "no attention is paid [among the brothers] to differences in talent or degrees of worthiness" but "all see themselves as servants in the temple of a sacred and sanctifying art," so that "the highest standpoint any one can reach is not to aspire to be a master, but to aspire to be a disciple of the one Master."[39]

---

[37]See Klaus Lankheit, *Das Freundschaftsbild der Romantik* (Heidelberg: Carl Winter Universitätsverlag, 1952), 90-92; Nikolaus Pevsner, "Gemeinschaftsideale unter den bildenden Künstlern des 19. Jahrhunderts," *Deutsche Vierteljahrsschrift für Literaturwissenschaft und Geistesgeschichte*, 1931, 9:124-54; Hans-Joachim Mähl, "Der poetische Staat: Utopie und Utopiereflexion bei den Frühromantikern," in Wilhelm Vosskamp, ed., *Utopieforschung: Interdisziplinäre Studien zur neuzeitlichen Utopie*, 3 vols. (Stuttgart: J.B. Metzler, 1982), 3:273-302. According to Mähl, "[Friedrich] Schlegel's social utopia refers first and foremost to the small circles of private life (and thus to groups of 'initiates,' which, like the Jena Romantic Circle itself, could be viewed as a new kind of 'community'). The 'invisible Church' evoked by Schlegel and so many others at this time should be understood as standing in opposition to the prevailing forms of society and was to be realized in the first instance in the form of a league of artists, since it was from artists that . . . the redemption of the world was expected to come" (p. 290).

[38]Howitt, 1:421.

[39]Büttner (as in note 8), p. 21. According to the painter Louise Seidel, who took part in common drawing exercises with other artists, the egalitarianism of the Lukasbrüder came to be characteristic of the entire German artists' colony in Rome during the period of the Nazarenes' greatest influence: "No one was appointed to be Director; what was formed was a little artists' republic; the painters themselves took over the not very pleasant chore of serving as models for each other in drapery drawing practice. No one begged off. I was enormously proud of the fact that, as the only woman, I was allowed to participate. Indeed this spurred me on to greater efforts. All in all, life in Rome was generally marked by a strong sense of comradeship." ["Kein Direktor war dazu ernannt; es bildete sich eine kleine Künstlerrepublik; die Maler selbst übernahmen die wahrlich nicht angenehme Mühe, einander gegenseitig zur Draperie zu stehen. Keiner schloss sich aus. Dass ich, die einzige Frau daran Theil nehmen durfte, erfüllte mich mit Stolz und spornte meinen Fleiss. Das Leben in Rom war überhaupt im Grossen und Ganzen durchaus kamaradschaftlich."] (*Erinnerungen und Leben der Malerin Louise Seidler* [as in note 24,] p. 264).

III

Both Overbeck and Pforr brought a number of started canvases or ideas for paintings with them to Rome and completed them there. Thus Pforr brought his *Entry of Rudolf of Habsburg into Basel in 1273* with him, and finished it in Rome. Overbeck had already inserted portraits of Pforr among the secondary figures in two earlier paintings – *The Raising of Lazarus* (1808) and *Christ's Entry into Jerusalem* (1809) **(Pf. 7)**. He began his *Portrait of Franz Pforr*, now one of his best-known compositions, on arriving in Rome in 1810, but broke off work on it on Pforr's death from tuberculosis in 1812. The final touches were not made to it until near the end of his life, in 1865, but the informed opinion is that they were not significant and that the painting was essentially finished at the time of Pforr's death. I shall take a short look at both works, in order to convey an idea of what Nazarene painting was like around 1812 and what the *Lukasbrüder*, the core constituency of the more heterogeneous movement referred to as the Nazarenes, were trying to do.

Overbeck's portrait of Pforr **(Fig. III, Pf. 8)** is a young artist's tribute to his friend, a monument to their friendship and artistic collaboration, and a vision of the artist as conceived by the Nazarenes. It contrasts strikingly with most portraits of the late eighteenth and early nineteenth centuries, not only late rococo works but even works by artists who had turned against the rococo and adopted a more severe neoclassical style **(Pf. 9, 10)**. Its aim is clearly not to produce, like most portraits of the time, a lively and appealing image of the subject and to *represent* the latter's social status and persona by the most sensuous possible depiction of dress, background, flesh tints, gesture, expression, and so on, but to *signify* the subject's essential character, values, and commitments. The incorrect, nongeometric perspective, with its flat receding planes, effectively excludes any impression of illusionist space. The relations among the pictorial elements, in other words, do not mirror empirical physical reality, but point to another, immaterial reality and the emphasis, instead of being on the optical experience of things, persons, and situations, is on the enduring spiritual essence that lies behind experience and is visible only to the inner eye. The eyes are certainly the dominant feature of Overbeck's Pforr, but while they look outward directly and seriously at the viewer, they do not seek

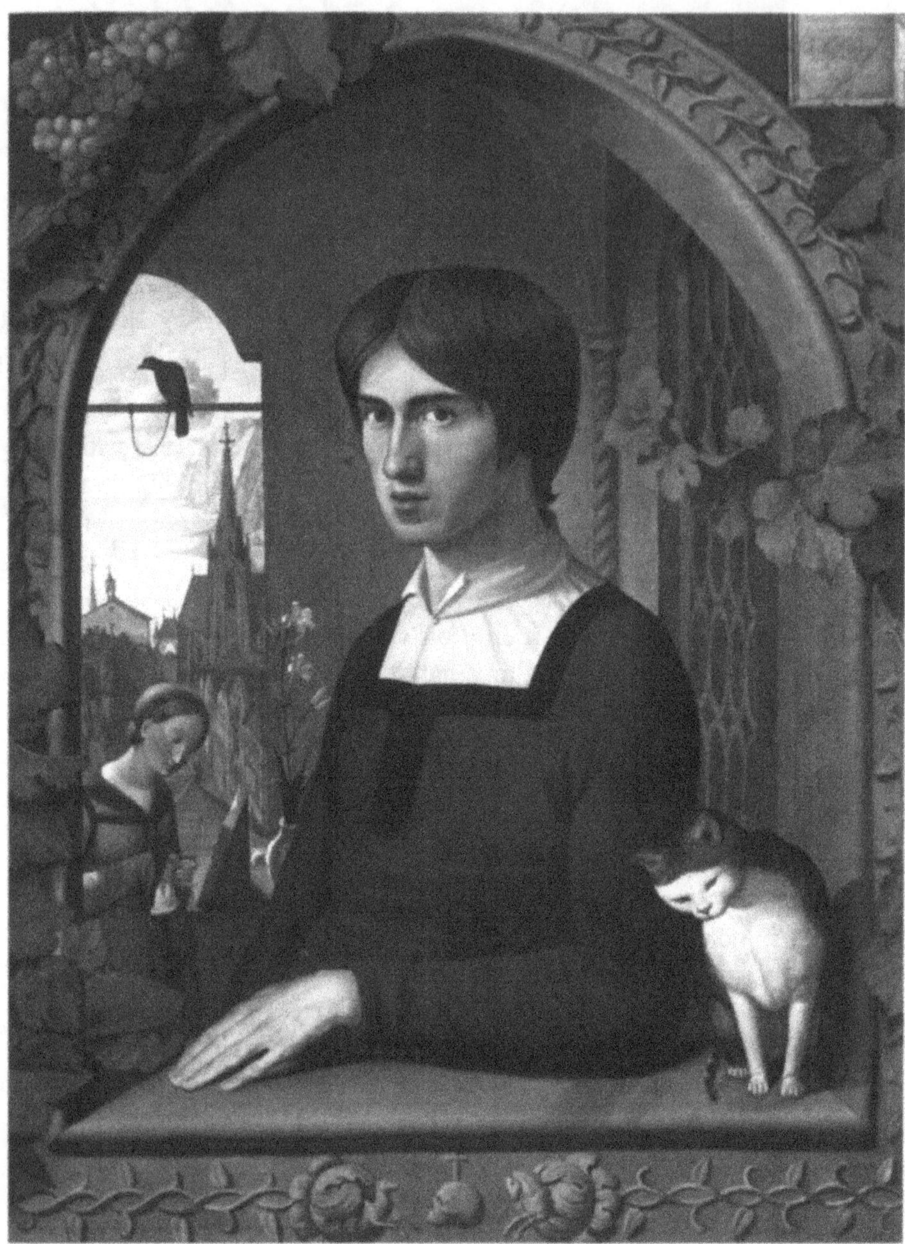

Fig. III. Friedrich Overbeck. *Bildnis des malers Franz Pforr.* (1810). Oil on canvas. 62 × 47 cm. Berlin, Staatliche Museen, Alte Nationalgalerie. Inv. No. A II 381. http://commons.wikimedia.org/wiki/Image:Friedrich_Overbeck_010 (The Yorck Project/GFDL)

to establish complicity with the viewer, as in many rococo portraits, and there seems to be no attempt to manipulate the viewer's reaction. The stillness of the composition, the firmness of the lines, and the absence of familiar illusionist depth hold the viewer at a certain distance and oblige him or her to decipher the portrait for himself or herself. Paradoxically, the effect of the old German costume and of the historical anachronism of style and setting is also to erase the entire question of historical reality and to emphasize that what the artist has aimed to provide is not an impression of his subject as a recognizable empirical presence but a vision of his subject both in his unique spiritual individuality and as the epitome of the Christian artist. Even the sitter's gender is not clearly represented by physical traits or dress: Overbeck's Pforr is very far from being a clothed male nude of the type students drew from models in the academies. He may in fact strike us as quite androgynous. Gender is at best *signified* by the implied relation to the equally idealized fair-haired female figure in a different part of the picture reading – Madonna-like – in an open book as she knits. Even so, there is virtually no sexual charge in the painting and it is clear from the representation of Pforr that male and female are not being construed here as radically different or mutually exclusive.

In creating his female figure Overbeck carefully followed the description Pforr himself had once given him of his ideal spouse: "a young, beautiful, fairhaired, tender, and extremely appealing maiden, simply but tastefully attired; . . . in short, such a maiden as Germany might have produced in the Middle Ages."[40] Far from being based on a live model, the figure was in all probability inspired by the same sources from which Pforr developed his ideal image of his bride – that is, pictures of the Virgin by old German masters such as Dürer or Martin Schongauer **(Pf. 11, 12)**. Some similarities to a stamp that Overbeck had devised for the certificate of membership of the *Lukasbund* and that was also intended to be applied to the back of canvases by the brothers who won the approval of the other members of the *Bund* **(Fig. IV, Pf. 13)** – the arched framing of the portrait, for instance, or the view of a steep Mediterranean coastline through the window at top left – may well have been intended to suggest an identification of Pforr with the patron saint of the *Lukasbrüder.* Pforr himself had associated the artistic vocation and the religious one: "I would ask anyone planning to dedicate himself to art the same question one would ask of someone who wanted to be a monk," he had declared. That is: " 'Can you take vows of poverty, chastity, and obedience and keep them?' If so, you are welcome."[41]

The idea that the image of Pforr was intended to convey the sacred character of art and the qualities of purity and dedication required of the artist is supported

[40]Quoted by Brigitte Heise, "Sulamith und Maria – ein Beispiel romantischer Sympoesie," in *Johann Friedrich Overbeck: Italia und Germania* (as in note 8), p. 38.

[41]Letter of 15.12.1810, quoted by Fastert (as in note 21), p. 38.

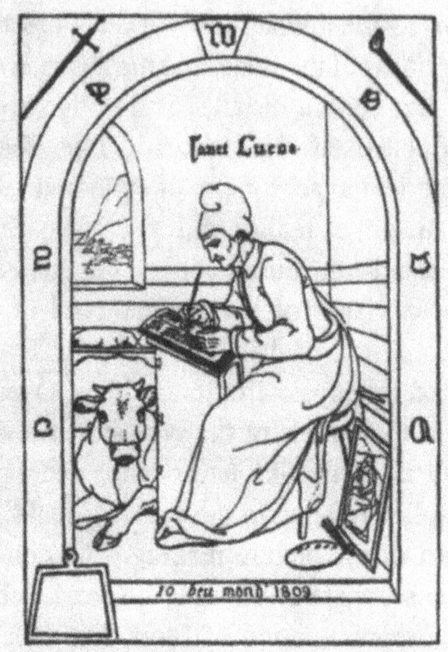

Fig. IV. Friedrich Overbeck. *Stamp of the Brotherhood of St. Luke.* Reproduced in Margaret Howitt, *Friedrich Overbeck: Sein Leben und Schaffen, nach seinen Briefen und anderen Dokumenten des handschriftlichen Nachlasses*, 2 vols (Freiburg: Herder'sche Verlagsbuchhandlung, 1886), vol. 1, facing p. 100.

by the wine-red of Pforr's garment, a color which, according to the color symbolism worked out by the two friends in Vienna, alluded to the Eucharist and was supposed to communicate a feeling of holiness. The coloring of the woman appears likewise to have been chosen to signify gentleness. Pforr himself had once noted that the artist should not use color simply to create sensuously pleasing effects but only in order "to produce a harmony of the individual being represented and his or her clothing."[42] The saintly, religious meaning of the image and the scene is further reinforced by the lily and the lectern beside the woman, both characteristic attributes of the Virgin. Other symbolic elements also point away from any realist or illusionist intention: the vine (signifying friendship [**Fig. III, top**]), the cat (a frequent presence in Pforr's work, linked here by the slanting line of the sitter's bust to the female figure on his right and thus perhaps identifiable as "il gatto della Madonna" – the symbol of maleficence disarmed and transformed by the Virgin), the domesticated falcon (used by Pforr in his illustrations for Goethe's play *Götz von Berlichingen* and

[42]Quoted in Lehr (as in note 21), p. 275; Fastert (as in note 21), p. 56. On the cat in the portrait, see Helmut Nickel, "The Bride and the Cat: A Possible Source for Overbeck's *Freunschaftbild* of Franz Pforr," *Metropolitan Museum Journal*, 27 (1992): 183-87.

applied here probably in its traditional meanings of hope and of the gentile converted to Christianity), the juxtaposition of a medieval German townscape and an Italian coastline (signifying the central theme for Overbeck and Pforr of the union of Raphael and Dürer, Italia and Germania, and, at the same time, the theme of their own friendship) as well as the engravings on the stonework of the frame within a frame, which include Pforr's personal emblem of a skull topped by a cross (the victory of faith over death).

Franz Pforr's historical painting, the *Entry of Rudolf of Habsburg into Basel in 1273,* begun in Vienna and completed in Rome in 1810, shortly after the brothers' arrival there, is no less radical in its defiance of contemporary norms than Overbeck's portrait **(Fig. V [see also color plate opposite p. 36], Pf. 14)**. The obvious reference to fifteenth- and sixteenth-century German painting and to the popular tradition of *Bilderbogen* – with their single woodcut sheets depicting tournaments, processions, and battles in uncompromisingly flat, two-dimensional design; their flat, heraldic, local colors applied in pattern one next to the other; and their hard, decisive contours – underlines the deliberate, conscious rejection of the illusionist tradition[43] and forces the modern

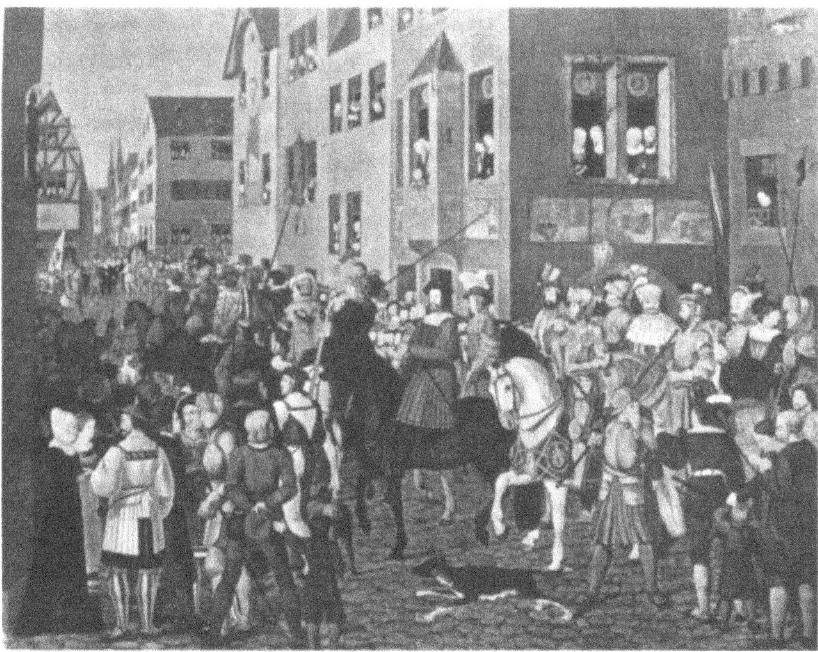

Fig. V. Franz Pforr. *Der Einzug König Rudolfs von Hapsburg in Basel 1273.* (1808-10). Oil on canvas. 90.5 × 118.9 cm. Frankfurt am Main, Städel Museum, Leihgabe des Historischen Museums.

[43]On Pforr's "Entry of Rudolf of Habsburg" as a "deliberate provocation aimed at the painting of the period," see Michel Le Bris, *Romantics and Romanticism* (Geneva: Skira; New York: Rizzoli, 1981), 96.

viewer to approach the work in a completely different spirit, to read it in a different way from that to which he or she has become accustomed. Although a certain suggestion of space is created by the turn of the procession into the street leading to the square in the middle left, which a welcoming party of burghers of Basel is about to enter from a narrow street "beyond," the rejection of correct geometric perspective and the seemingly arbitrary relative proportions of buildings and figures effectively block any naturalistic illusion. The line of the houses *signifies* depth, but the buildings are *perceived* as stretched across the flat surface of the painting. In the terms Robert Rosenblum used about the neoclassical artist Jacob Asmus Carstens (who, as it happens, was supported financially for a time by Overbeck's father), Pforr's painting communicates "an idea of a space, rather than an illusion of space."[44]

As the dominant formal element in the work, contour gives to every part of it a precise definition, allowing the figures, despite a certain degree of plasticity, to be integrated into the surface plane. The impression of a bright surface image, with no illusionist ambitions, is reinforced by Pforr's application of color, which is always firmly contained within the precise contours of figures and buildings, by the typically Old German accuracy of detail, and by the absence of light effects. The even distribution of light also prevents the subordination of any one part of the painting to any other. At the same time, the figure of Rudolf is given special importance by being placed at the center of the picture, where the diagonals formed by the groups on the left and the right intersect and the procession shifts direction – in a movement indicated by a slight inclination of Rudolf's horse's head. The artist's use of color also focuses attention on Rudolf as the strikingly colorless, grey central point of the entire bright pageant.

If the painting does not aim to create an illusion of reality, it also does not aspire to historical or antiquarian realism. Never having been to Basel, Pforr asked his childhood friend, the artist and art historian David Passavant, to describe the Rathaus there to him and Passavant sent him a sketch of it. Pforr thanked him, but explained that he "could not make use of it because the architectural style was not appropriate."[45] Instead, Pforr appears to have found inspiration for the street scene and the architecture in German illustrations of the late fifteenth and early sixteenth century. Likewise, the dress of the figures in the picture is not that of 1273 but that of the early sixteenth century. Pforr's intention, in short, appears to have been to create neither a visually realistic nor a historically accurate image, but a symbolical one, exploring and exhibiting the meaning of the event depicted.[46] Picking up on Schiller's ballad

[44]Robert Rosenblum, *The International Style of 1800. A Study in Linear Abstraction* (New York and London: Garland Publishing, 1976; Ph.D. Thesis, New York University, April 1956), p. 96.

[45]"Es ging aber wegen der Bauarth nicht gut an, es gebrauchen zu können" (quoted in Lehr [as in note 19], p.108; Fastert [as in note 21], p. 74).

[46]See Fastert (as in note 21), pp. 73-74.

on the subject, Pforr had already painted the legendary episode of *Rudolf of Habsburg and the Priest* (1808-1809) **(Pf. 15)** – in which Rudolph dismounts from his horse and helps a priest carrying the sacraments to a sick person to cross a stream. As the Habsburgs were widely considered the chief defenders of German independence against Napoleon in those years, this subject had achieved great popularity[47] and was painted over and over again in the first four decades of the nineteenth century (by fellow Nazarene artists Ferdinand Olivier [1816] and Josef Wintergerst [1822], a special friend of Pforr's, among others). Rudolf came to symbolize the good monarch, modest, compassionate, helpful, and, as a bringer of peace and order, a particular friend of burghers and townspeople – a German anticipation of the *roi bourgeois*. Pforr's "Entry" has thus to be read not as a realistic portrayal of an historical moment or event but as a portrayal of its meaning. The grey of the Emperor's costume at the center of the colorful painting, for instance, signifies the hero's legendary modesty.

A well-developed series of wall paintings within the painting is likewise richly significant, rather than merely serving as historical *couleur locale*. On the furthest wall of the first row of houses on the right, a large painting of St. Christopher (who, according to legend, carried Christ [*Christum ferit*] in the form of a child, across a river) serves as a prefiguration of the story of Rudolf and the Priest. A further series of smaller wall paintings stretching from just beyond the first oriel window on the right to the extreme right of the painting depicts episodes from the Old Testament story of Joseph in Egypt: the furthest away, largely concealed by the protruding window, most likely Joseph being sold into slavery by his brothers; the next, Joseph resisting Potiphar's wife; the next again, Joseph interpreting the dreams of the chief butler and the chief baker in prison; then, on the wall parallel to the picture surface, Joseph interpreting Pharaoh's dream of the lean and the fat kine and being made governor of Egypt; and finally, Joseph's recognition by his brothers **(Fig. VI, Pf. 16)**.

From early Christian times, Joseph in Egypt had commonly been interpreted as a figure of Christ: as Joseph was sold into slavery, then thrown into prison, then raised by Pharaoh to rule over Egypt, and finally reunited with his brothers, so Christ was betrayed by Judas, then crucified and buried, then resurrected to rule with his Father, and reunited with his Church. By the high

[47]August Wilhelm Schlegel, for instance, compiled and published a collection of poems about Rudolf – "Gedichte auf Rudolf von Habsburg von Zeitgenossen" – in 1812. (See *Dorothea Schlegel, geb. Mendelssohn und deren Söhne Johannes und Philipp Veit: Briefwechsel* [as in note 25], 2:77, letter dated 16.5.1812). Nearly two decades earlier, Friedrich Schlegel had urged his brother to write a biography of Rudolf and claimed he had contemplated such a project himself (*Friedrich Schlegels Briefe an seinen Bruder August Wilhelm*, Oskar F. Walzel, ed. [Berlin: Speyer & Peters, 1890], p. 202, letter dated 7.12.1794). August Wilhelm apparently had misgivings, having concluded that Rudolf was more concerned with personal and dynastic success than with the political fortunes of the Empire and that he should be viewed as an outstanding example of knighthood rather than an exemplary Emperor (Otto Brandt, *A.W. Schlegel. Der Romantiker und die Politik* [Stuttgart and Berlin: Deutsche Verlagsanstalt, 1919], pp. 61-63).

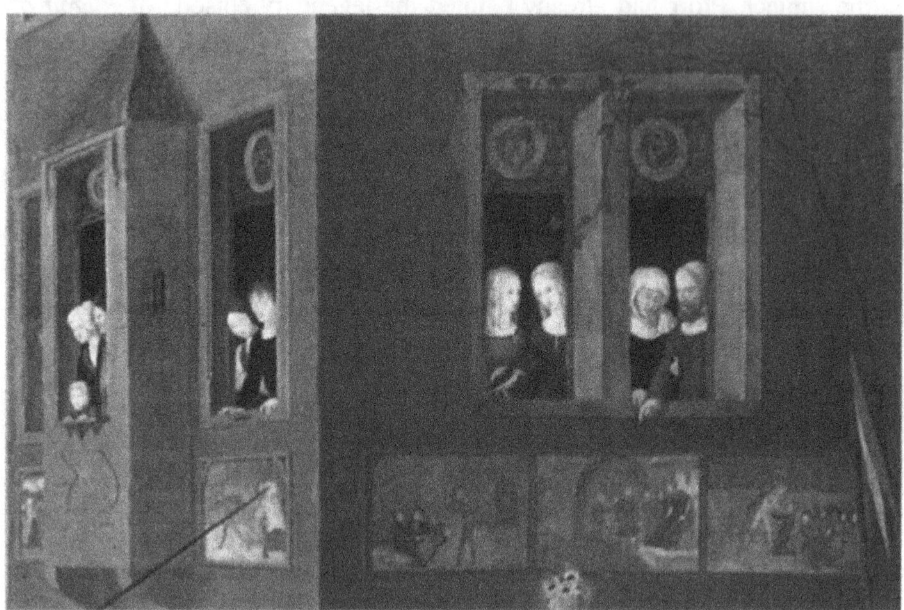

Fig. VI. Franz Pforr. *Der Einzug König Rudolfs von Hapsburg in Basel 1273* (detail).

Middle Ages, the figuration had been extended to encompass secular rulers, as in the Sainte-Chapelle in Paris, where the Joseph story alludes to the piety, justice, and generosity of Louis IX (Saint-Louis), the royal donor. In Pforr's painting, the scene of Joseph being elevated to governor of Egypt, to which the viewer is directed by the pointing index finger of the bearded man in the last but one window on the right, prefigures the election of Rudolf as Emperor, which has just occurred at the time represented in the picture and which Rudolf is marking by forgiving an offence against him by the burghers of Basel. Far from being the illusionist representation of a singular moment of history (as the specificity of the date might lead one to expect), *The Entry of Rudolf of Habsburg into Basel in 1273* has a temporal dimension that extends from the Joseph story of the Old Testament through the life of Christ and the legend of St. Christopher to the election of Rudolf of Habsburg in 1273 and, beyond that historical moment, to the period in the style of which the artist has constructed the scene (the early sixteenth century), the role of the Habsburgs as German Emperors until Napoleon's dissolution of the Empire in 1806, and the widespread hope of the artist's own generation that a new, wise, peace-loving emperor would unite the German nation and liberate it from the Napoleonic yoke.[48]

Overbeck's fondness for representing his fellow artists and members of his family among the secondary figures in his religious paintings, such as the

[48]See Wilhelm Schlink, "Heilsgeschichte in der Malerei der Nazarener," *Aurora: Jahrbuch der Eichendorff-Gesellschaft*, n. 61 (Stuttgart: Jan Thorbecke, 2001), pp. 97–118.

Entry of Christ into Jerusalem, or even directly as a particular Biblical figure, as in the pencil drawing *Ruth and Boas* of 1818 **(Pf. 17)**, where Ruth has the traits of his new wife Nina (in fact, the drawing was intended to be sent to Lübeck in order to introduce Nina to his parents),[49] bears witness to a similar figural or typological rather than naturalistic view of history and was in fact vigorously denounced by the critics of Nazarene painting.[50] Comparison with the work of other contemporary history painters brings out the originality of the Nazarenes in this respect **(Pf. 18)**. Thus a painting that Robert Rosenblum compared with Pforr's *Entry* – the Frenchman Pierre-Henri Revoil's *The Tournament*, exhibited at the salon of 1812 – lacks this specific historical dimension. The historical reference here is no more than formal and picturesque **(Pf. 19)**.

Among the works that Pforr and Overbeck took up in Rome around 1810 were a number of drawings on two closely related themes: their idea of art and the artist's vocation, and their own friendship and collaboration. For the first – the idea of art and the artist's vocation – they were inspired by Wilhelm Heinrich Wackenroder's fictitious account in his immensely popular *Herzensergiessungen eines kunstliebenden Klosterbruders* (1797) of a meeting between Albrecht Dürer and Sanzo Raphael, the leading representatives of Northern or German Renaissance art and of Southern or Italian Renaissance art. A drawing by Pforr, known to us from an edition of eleven drawings that the Frankfurt Kunstverein had engraved and published 20 years after the artist's death at Overbeck's instigation, portrays Dürer (on the viewer's left) and Raphael (on the right) kneeling before the throne of "die heilige Kunst" (Holy Art), which is represented by a figure hardly distinguishable from the Virgin **(Fig. VII, Pf. 20)**. The accompanying description in the Frankfurt Kunstverein edition, which, if not by Overbeck himself, must at least have been approved by him, reads: "An allegorical composition by means of which the artist wished to convey his idea of the task of modern art – namely, to bring about the synthesis of Old German and Old Italian art. Albrecht Dürer and Raphael kneeling before the throne of Art, who is noting down for a future age their names and the services they have rendered. In the background Nuremberg and Rome."

Overbeck's drawing on the same theme, now in the Albertina in Vienna and unfortunately quite faded, switches the positions of Raphael and Dürer **(Fig. VIII, Pf. 21)**. Raphael is now on the viewer's left, his head crowned by a laurel wreath – like the later figure of Italia – and Dürer is on the right, crowned by a wreath of oak leaves. Raphael is offering the figure of Art a

---

[49]*Die Nazarener*, Catalogue of Exhibition, Städtische Galerie in Städelschen Institut, Frankfurt am Main, April–August 1977, ed. Klaus Gallwitz, pp. 152–53, 201; *Johann Friedrich Overbeck* 1789–1869. Zur zweihundertsten Wiederkeh, seines Geburtstages, Catalogue of Exhibition, Museum für Kunst und Kulturgeschichte der Hausestadt Lübeck, June–September 1989, Andreas Blühm and Gerhard Kerkens, eds., pp. 205, 208.

[50]E.g., by Salomon Bartholdy, the Nazarenes' first patron, in a critical review of an exhibition of work by German artists in Rome in 1819, *Beilage zur Allgemeine Zeitung*, 23.7.1819, No. 124, p. 495, col. 1.

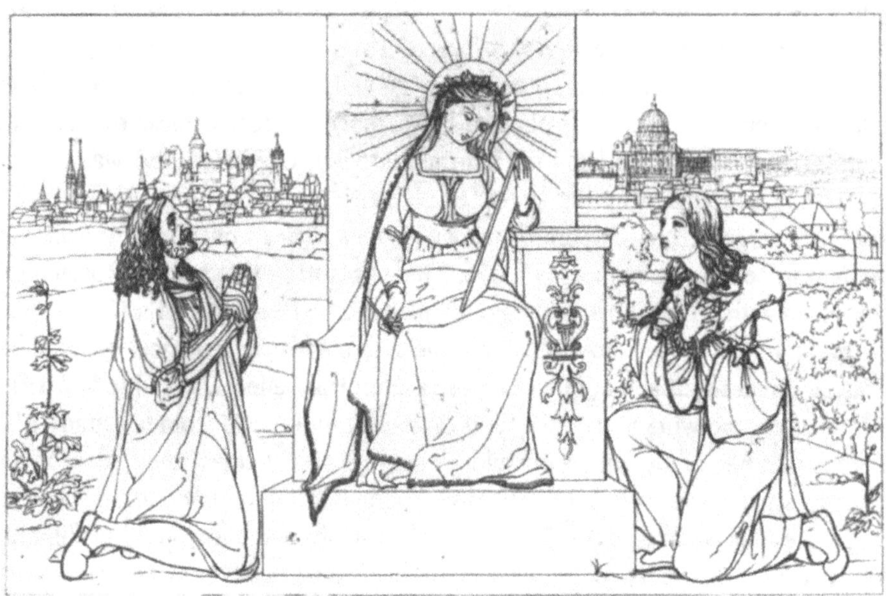

Fig. VII. Franz Pforr. *Dürer und Raffael vor dem Throne der Kunst.* (Circa 1810). Etching by Carl Hoff (1807-1862) after an original drawing, now lost. In *Compositionen und Handzeichnungen aus dem Nachlass von Franz Pforr*, published by Kunstverein zu Frankfurt a. M., Part 1 (1832), No.1. 13.7 × 21.4 cm. Reproduced in Fritz Herbert Lehr, *Die Blütezeit romantischer Bildkunst: Franz Pforr, der Meister des Lukasbundes* (Marburg: Verlag des kunstgeschichtlichen Seminars der Universität Marburg an der Lahn, 1924), Tafel XXX, Abb. 62.

picture of the Madonna (hard to see) and Dürer a picture of the Crucifixion (a little easier to make out). The figure of Art clearly represents Christian Art and beyond that the ultimate object of the artists' veneration: the Virgin and Christ himself. She sits on a bishop's throne, her tiara has the form of a crown of thorns, there is a bishop's staff on her right, and she wears a large pectoral cross. In a direct allusion to Wackenroder's text, which described "Raphael und Albrecht Dürer Hand in Hand," and in anticipation of an essential motif of the later *Sulamith und Maria* or *Italia und Germania*, the clasped hands of Raphael and Dürer are at the center of Overbeck's drawing.

Let us turn now to the friendship drawings. Overbeck relates that at one point he had the idea that "each of them should paint a picture for the other that would display the essential beauty and character of his particular style of art." These were to be conveyed "by two female figures, representing the tradition in painting that each had chosen."[51] The two friends would apparently

[51] "Es sollte jeder für den anderen ein Bild malen, in welchem die wesentliche Schönheit und der Charakter der Jedem eigenthümlichen Kunstweise zur Erscheinung kommen müsste; dieselben könnten, meinte er, ganz wohl durch zwei Frauengestalten, als Repräsentanten der beiden von ihnen erwählten 'Arten der Malerei' dargestellt werden" (quoted by Howitt, 1:196).

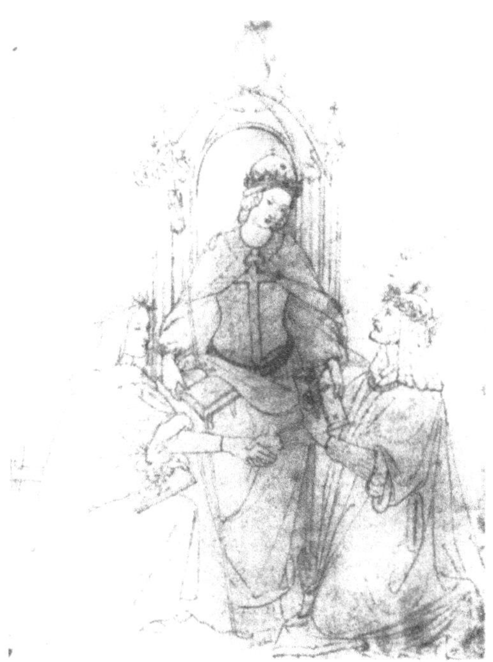

Fig. VIII. Friedrich Overbeck. *Raffael und Dürer vor dem Throne der Kunst.* (Circa 1810). Pencil. 25.5 × 20 cm. Unsigned. Vienna, Graphische Sammlung Albertina. Inv. No. 23.694.

gaze on their sketches for hours at a time and on one occasion, Overbeck asked Pforr teasingly if he had perhaps fallen in love with his ideal female.[52] As a result of that question, the two female figures came to represent both each young man's idea of art and his ideal bride. It did not take much for the two figures to be invested with still more, related meanings. In addition to the bride as Art and the bride as future spouse, the two females could also readily represent the bride of Christ – in the form, on the one hand, of the Virgin and, on the other of her Old Testament prefiguration, the Shulamite bride of Solomon – as well as the artists themselves, inasmuch as they felt themselves to be betrothed to Art and to Christ. The association of the two females could thus symbolize not only the collaboration of old Italian and old German art, but the friendship of the two artists and the support each gave to the other in their common pursuit of a beloved that was at once Art, Holy Church, the Redeemer, and a longed-for incarnation of these in a real human being.[53] By choosing to represent their friendship through two female figures – and, in addition to its

[52]Brigitte Heise (as in note 40), p. 38.

[53]See Gisela Scheffler, "Zum neuerworbenen Karton 'Italia und Germania' der Staatlichen Graphischen Sammlung München," Introduction to *Johann Friedrich Overbeck: Italia und Germania* (as in note 8), pp. 12, 13; Büttner (as in note 8), p. 19.

central role in the well-known *Italia und Germania* of Overbeck and in the small, delicate *Sulamith und Maria* that Pforr painted, toward the end of his short life, as a personal gift for Overbeck **(Fig. IX, [see also color plate opposite p. 37] Pf. 22)**, this private symbolism makes a discreet appearance in several other works by both artists **(Figs. X, XI, Pf. 23, 24)** – Overbeck and Pforr were clearly investing it with a different range of meanings from those that would have been suggested by the more common heroic male figures of Achilles and Patroclus or David and Jonathan.

Pforr appears to have begun the friendship series with an *Allegorie der Freundschaft*, which he drew in 1808 when he and Overbeck were still students at the Vienna Academy **(Fig. XII, Pf. 25)**. In it the two friends are represented by the ideals, artistic and personal, that had emerged in the course of their long evening conversations – an Italianate, Raphael-like figure in the case of

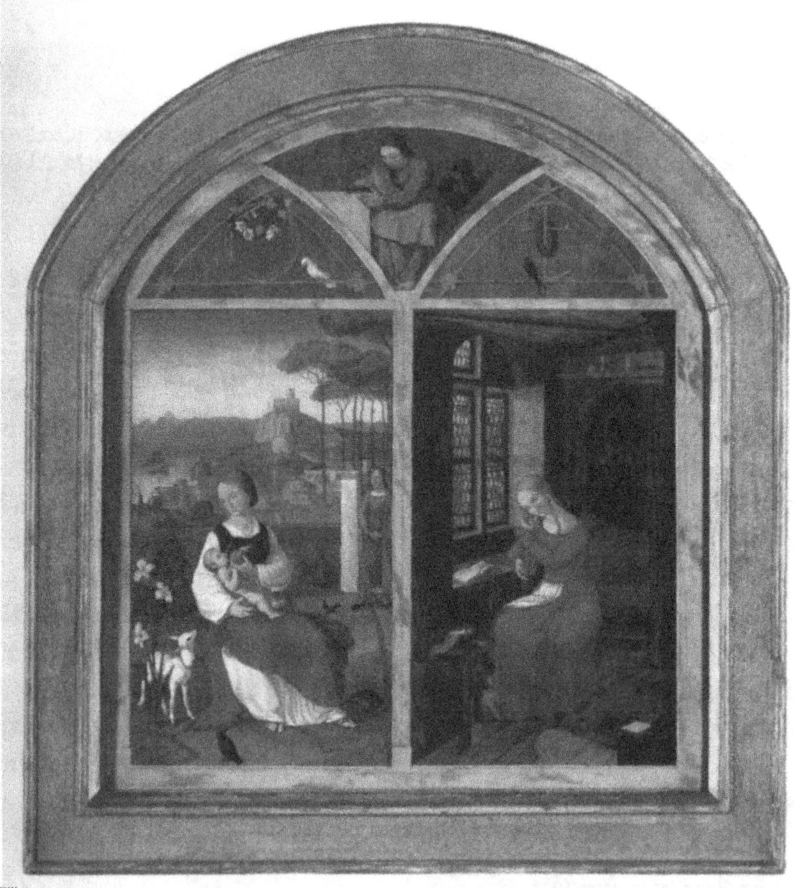

Fig. IX. Franz Pforr. *Sulamith und Maria.* (1811). Oil on wood. 34.5 × 32 cm. Unsigned. Schweinfurt, Museum Georg Schäfer. Inv. No. MGS 1183.

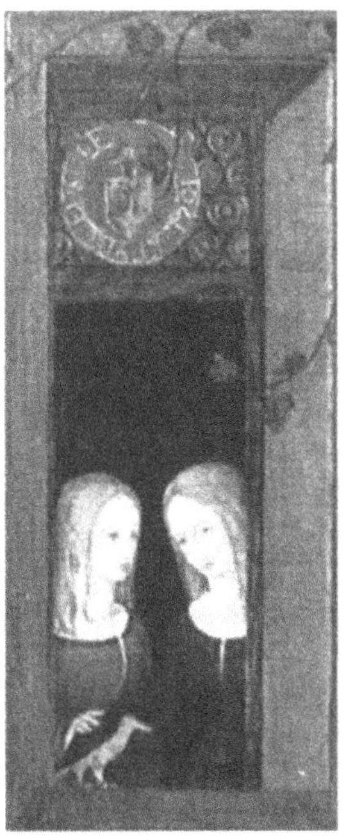

Fig. X. Franz Pforr. *Der Einzug König Rudolfs von Hapsburg in Basel 1273* (detail).

Overbeck (on the left) and a Germanic, Dürer-like figure, somewhat reminiscent of the famous Melancholia, in the case of Pforr (on the right). In Pforr's drawing the figure on the left clasps the hands of the other figure as though to console her. Melancholia (Pforr) is no longer alone, but now has a friend. As in Dürer's *Melancholia*, moreover, the central figures in Pforr's drawing are surrounded by allegorical objects. These point, on the one hand, to the qualities of friendship – fidelity (the dog), generosity (the open purse), everlastingness (the snake biting its tail), readiness to come to each other's aid (the sword) – and, on the other, to the basis of the two students' friendship in their common view that the renewal of art requires its reconsecration to the service of religion, that is, to the Christian faith and the Christian church. The image of the Last Supper, above the two figures, can be read as a Biblical exemplum of the brotherhood sworn to by Pforr and Overbeck (and doubtless confirmed by a shared meal). This picture within the picture thus identifies the friends as modern apostles preaching the gospel of a Christian art. In the left-hand section of the drawing an eagle looks toward a Church and the rising sun. As the eagle is, among other things, an attribute of John the Evangelist and as Overbeck's first name was Johannes – this was the name Pforr always used in speaking of him, whereas everybody else called him by his second name Friedrich or, in the family circle, Fritz – the symbolism is again of apostles united in their endeavor

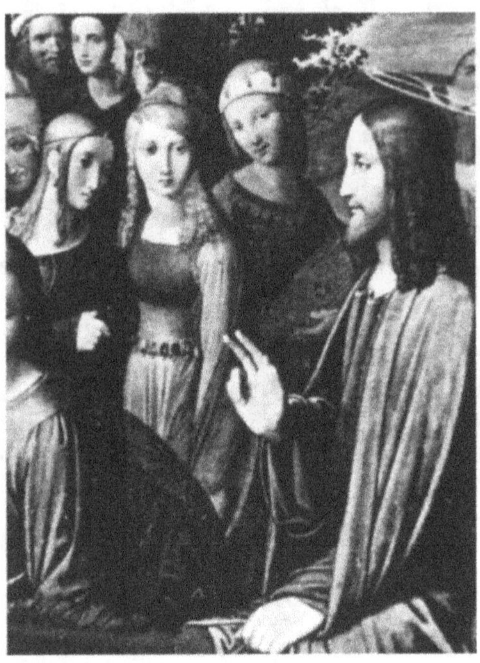

Fig. XI. Friedrich Overbeck. *Einzug Christi in Jerusalem (detail).* (1809/24). Oil on canvas. 157.6 × 229 cm. Originally in Lübeck Cathedral; destroyed during Second World War. (From a black-and-white reproduction in Kurt Karl Eberlein, *Die Malerei der deutschen Romantik und Nazarener im besonderen Overbecks und seines Kreises* (Munich: Kurt Wolff, 1928), Plate 5.

to rededicate art to the service of religion and "Truth." This reading is reinforced, moreover, by another traditional meaning of the eagle as the bird that can look directly at the sun and that flies up toward it in order to rejuvenate itself – an allusion no doubt not only to the personal "awakening" of the friends and the renewal of their faith but to the renewal of art through religion.[54]

In Overbeck's version of this same theme, Pforr's drawing, which the latter had given him as a token of their friendship, is still visibly present in the way the figures are turned to each other, in the clasped hands, and in the differentiating wreaths of laurel and oak that adorn each figure **(Fig. XIII, Pf. 26)**. But the composition has undergone significant changes. The two figures are now monumentalized, filling the entire canvas, like the figures in Overbeck's later madonna-and-child-like sketch for a portrait of his wife, Nina, and son, Alfonso, of 1820 or his family portrait of 1820-22 **(Pf. 27, 28)**, and the Dürer-like apparatus of symbolic objects has been eliminated. In addition, the two women are no longer clearly separated, each occupying a space of her own, but have been brought together to form the central pyramidal structure of the

[54]See Büttner (as in note 8), p. 28.

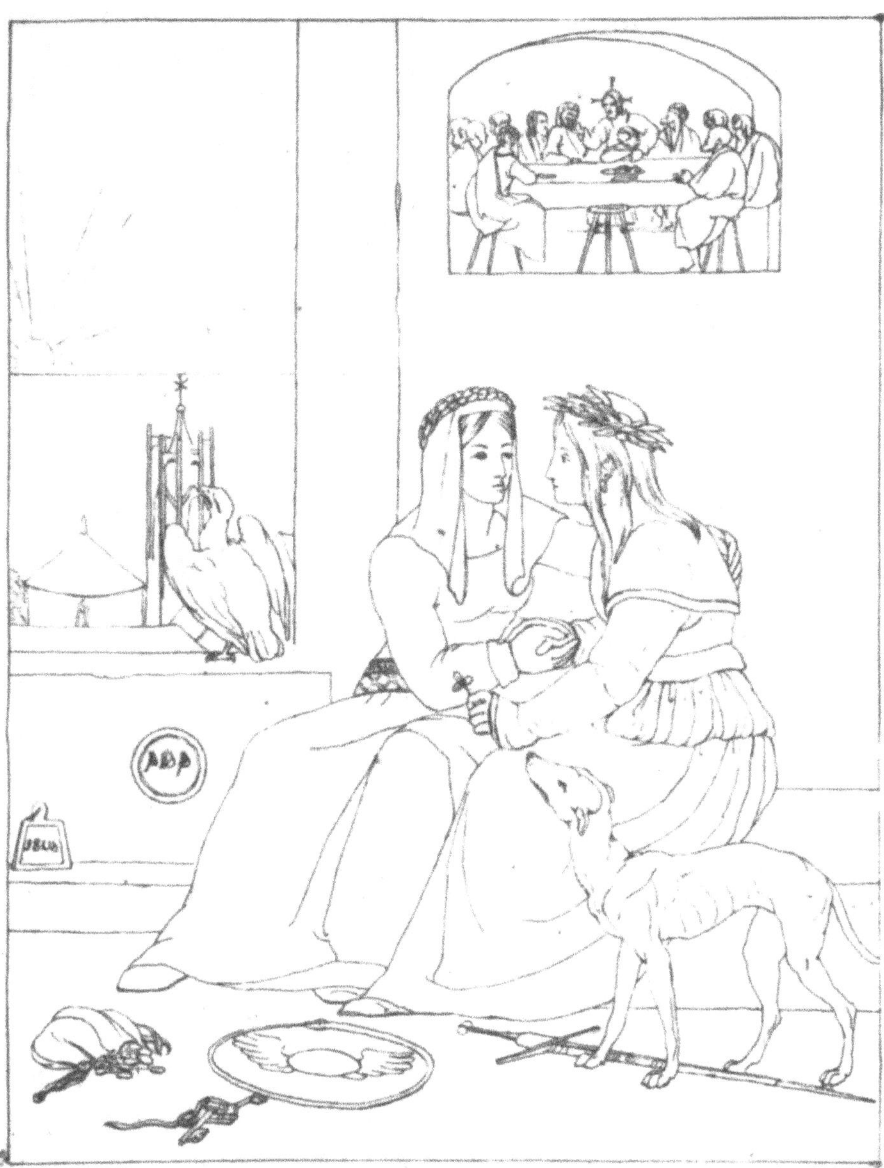

Fig. XII. Franz Pforr. *Allegorie der Freundschaft*. (1808). Pen and ink. 24.7 × 19.3 cm. Frankfurt am Main, Städel Museum.

image. As one scholar put it, Overbeck has "harmonized" the figures that Pforr presented – more markedly still in his diptych **(Fig. IX, Pf. 22)** than in the drawing – as complementary opposites.[55] Curiously, however, even though Pforr was now in failing health, already stricken by the tuberculosis that was

[55]Jens Christian Jensen, *Friedrich Overbeck. Die Werke im Behnhaus* (Lübeck, 1963; Lübecker Museumshefte, Heft 4), p. 22.

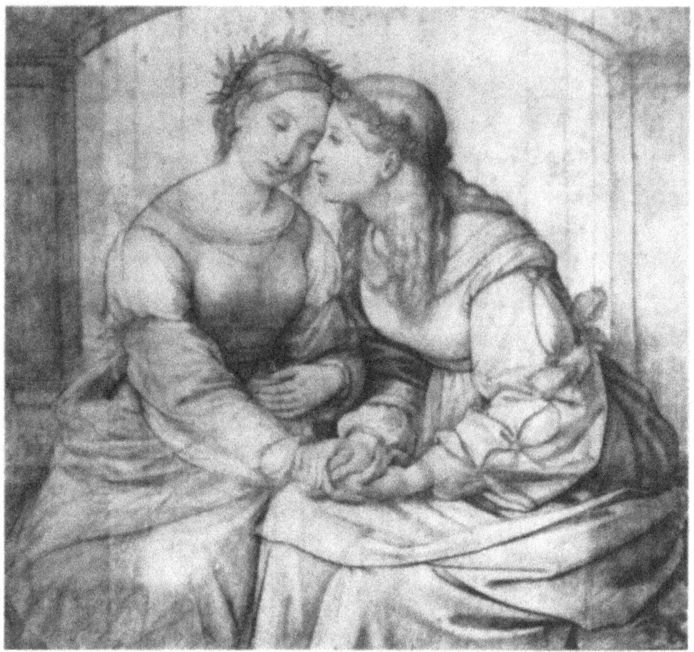

Fig. XIII. Friedrich Overbeck. *Sulamith und Maria.* (1812). Charcoal and black chalk on cardboard. 91.7 × 102.2 cm. Lübeck, Museum für Kunst und Kultur der Hansestadt Lübeck. Inv. Nr. AB 126.

to kill him a couple of years later, Overbeck makes the figure corresponding to Pforr the stronger and the more richly clad. As one or two critics have observed, it is as though the fair-haired figure on the right is offering encouragement and support to the rather downcast, dark-haired figure on the left with her lowered gaze and limp hands.[56] It is the right-hand figure in Overbeck's drawing, moreover, as later again in the painting, who takes the initiative and clasps the hands of the left-hand figure – another reversal of Pforr's design. In the latter, it is the left-hand figure that holds the right-hand figure's hands in hers. These differences may simply convey that each one of the friends felt the need of and was grateful for the encouragement and support offered by the other. Further exploration of Overbeck's reworking of Pforr's original plan, however, may provide a fuller interpretation of it.

[56]See Gisela Scheffler (as in note 53), pp. 13-14, 58; Büttner (as in note 8), p. 31. Likewise Wolfgang Pruscha in www.viaggio-in-germania.de/italia_over.html: "Germania is unequivocally the more active. It is she who has seized Italia's hand, bends toward her, and seems also to want to tell her something. Italia, to be sure, is slightly taller than Germania (as she has to be, since she is, after all, the embodiment of the Madonna) but she is distinctly passive. Almost shyly she holds back her left hand as if she did not want to yield that other hand also to Germania. Her glance is modestly downcast, whereas Germania's gaze is cast widely; she looks out of the picture and into the world. Italia, in contrast, seems turned inward and notably helpless; in addition, she has no wall, no support behind her. It seems as though Germania has to console Italia. . . . Despite the idealizing superiority in height attributed to Italy, Germany seems somehow to be the more dominant figure."

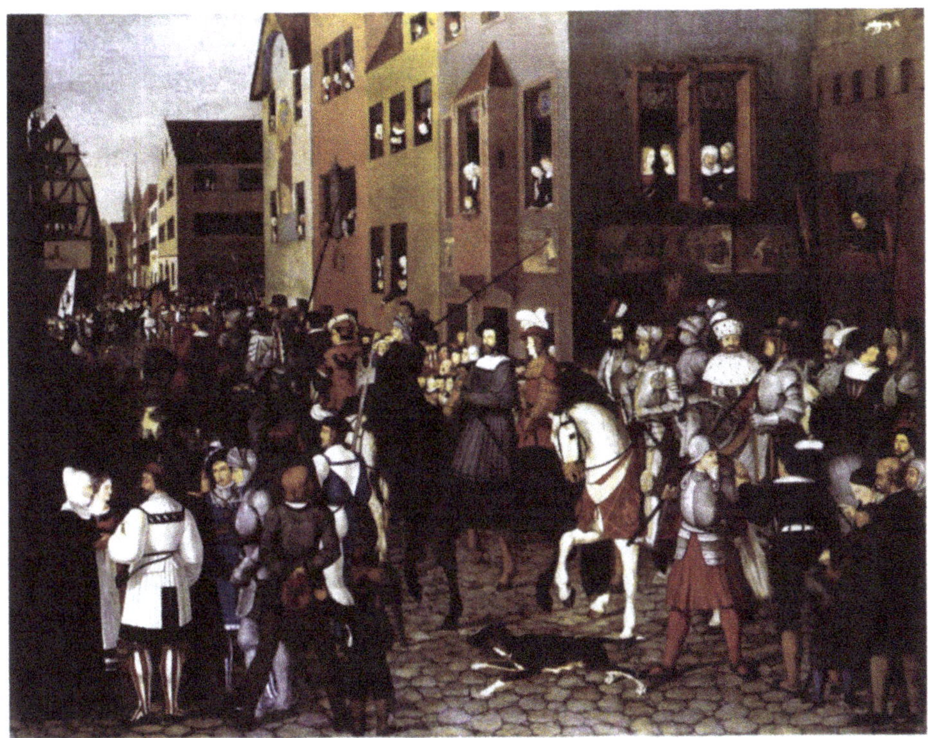

Fig. V. Franz Pforr. *Der Einzug König Rudolfs von Hapsburg in Basel 1273.* (1808-10). Oil on canvas. 90.5 × 118.9 cm. Frankfurt am Main, Städel Museum, Leihgabe des Historischen Museums.

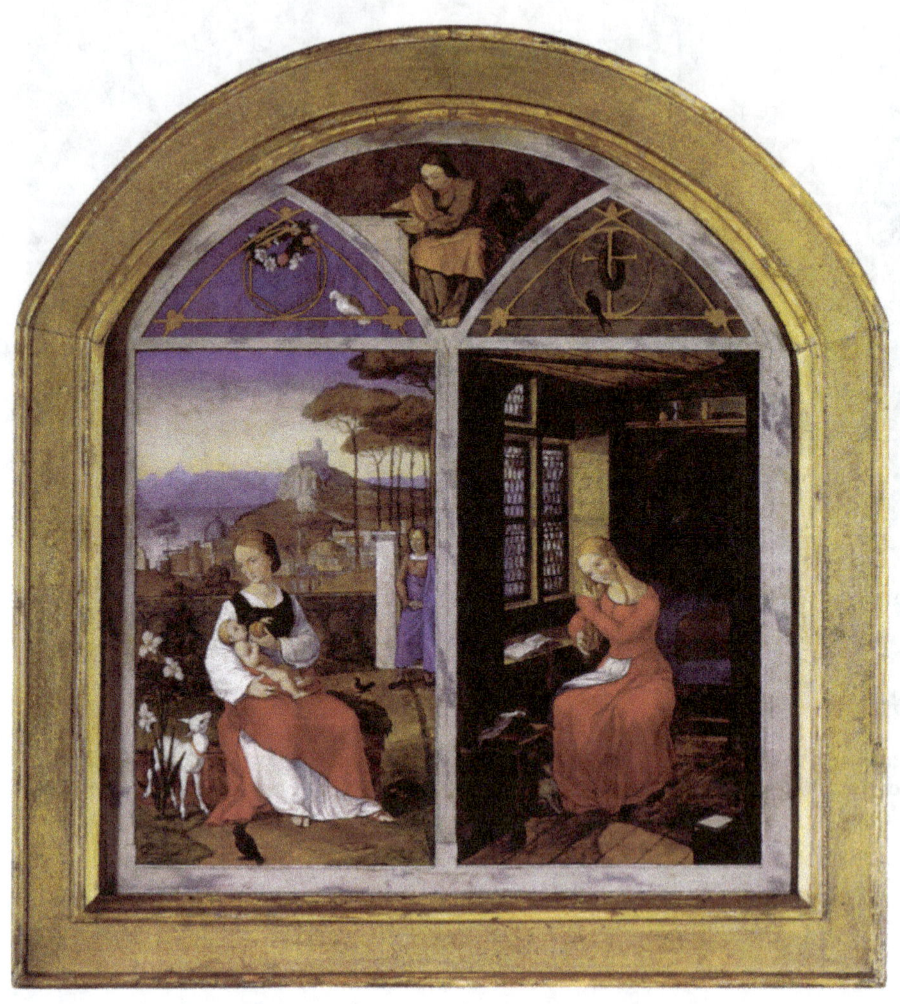

Fig. IX. Franz Pforr. ***Sulamith und Maria.*** (1811). Oil on wood. 34.5 × 32 cm. Unsigned. Schweinfurt, Museum Georg Schäfer. Inv. No. MGS 1183.

IV

An obvious first step would be to consider the names the two men gave to their two female figures. It was apparently Overbeck who came up with the idea of calling his ideal bride and artistic ideal "Sulamith," to which Pforr responded by choosing to give his the name "Maria." Pforr then proceeded to write a kind of fable in the style of a simple folk legend about two sisters "Sulamith und Maria," and later painted the lovely miniature, diptych-like canvas, entitled *Sulamith und Maria* **(Fig. IX, Pf. 22)**, as a gift for his friend – a parting gift, as it turned out, for he died shortly after completing it in 1814.

Pforr's fable cannot be ignored in any analysis of Overbeck's final painting and the following is a much abbreviated account of it. It tells of a couple, Joseph and Elizabeth, who lacked for nothing, except that after fourteen years of marriage they remained childless. Then one day they learned that their prayers had been answered and that miraculously, as it were, Elizabeth was with child. When the moment of delivery arrived, Joseph was anxious and took down his Bible to regain some calm. At the point where he opened it, his eyes lighted on the well-known passage of the Old Testament Song of Songs (6:13): "Return, return, O Shulamite" ["Kehre wieder, kehre wieder, o Sulamith" in German; "Revertere, revertere Sulamitis" in the Vulgate]. Immediately he was told that his wife had borne him a daughter, he knew that she should be named Sulamith. As the midwife asked him to wait a while longer, he opened the Bible at random again, this time at the passage in the New Testament Gospel of Luke (1:26-27) that tells of the Annunciation – how God sent the angel Gabriel "unto a city of Galilee named Nazareth, to a virgin espoused to a man whose name was Joseph . . . and the virgin's name was Mary." When the midwife announces to Joseph that his wife has borne him a second, twin daughter, he again understands immediately that she must be named Maria. Some years later, the Queen of the country sees the two daughters of Joseph and Elizabeth sitting outside their parents' house. She is struck by their beauty and grace and as she has no daughter of her own, she asks the King to allow her to adopt one of them and bring her to the palace to live with them. Though loth to part with a child they love dearly, Joseph and Elizabeth, knowing what it is to long for a child, believe it would be an act of great charity to do so. They consent, and Sulamith moves to the palace, where she lives like a princess, remaining, however, modest and unassuming in her heart. Though she does not care for finery, she is dressed in the finest clothes and wears the most beautiful jewels. On her visits home to her parents she tries to persuade Maria to accept some of her clothes and jewelry, but Maria, modest and retiring as befits a simple burgher's daughter, accepts almost nothing. Nor does she like to visit the palace. Then one day, the Queen falls ill and dies. Sulamith is allowed to return to her parents. The king insists, however, that she keep all the gifts of clothes and jewelry that the Queen had given her and that in memory of the Queen's great love for her, she also keep the crown, and wear it on holidays, even though it is a sign of royalty.

Joseph now has a dream that troubles him greatly. He dreams that he is sitting at a table with one daughter on his left and the other on his right, when suddenly a palm branch sprouts between him and Sulamith and a sprig of rosemary between him and Maria. He is deeply disturbed by this dream, interpreting it to mean that Sulamith will enjoy good fortune and happiness, the palm being a symbol of peace and prosperity, whereas Maria is destined to die young, rosemary being a symbol of death. (Pforr may well have given expression in this dream to his anticipation of his own early death.) The following day being Christmas Day, the Birthday of the Lord, Joseph and Elizabeth had invited two close friends as guests, but it turns out that they cannot come. As the couple has prepared a festive meal, they decide to invite any two strangers who pass by their house. Thus it happens that two traveling artists who had come to the town to paint pictures of the saints and episodes from the Holy Gospels join Joseph and Elizabeth and their two daughters for Christmas dinner. Noticing that each has a sign sown in silk on the front of his shirt, Joseph asks what the signs mean. "Why should we conceal it from you?" one of the artists responds. "You are like a father to us. We are brothers in a *Bund,* as members of which we have sworn to stay together through thick and thin and do everything in our power to improve our art. It is the custom among us artists that each one of us has such a sign" (as indeed all the members of the *Lukasbund* did, Overbeck's being a palm branch and Pforr's a skull topped by a cross). Joseph sees that the sign worn by one of the young men is a palm branch, that worn by the other a black cross atop a white skull. Joseph now understands the meaning of his dream, but says nothing. The two young men, whose names turn out to be Johannes (i.e., Overbeck's first name) and Albrecht (the first name of Dürer, thus signifying Pforr) come frequently to the house in the course of carrying out their commission in the town. One – not surprisingly, it is Johannes – falls in love with Sulamith, whereas the other, Albrecht – he of the skull topped by a cross – is drawn to the Maria of the sprig of rosemary. Johannes proposes to Sulamith in a garden where she liked to walk and where a vine has entwined itself around a palm tree. Sulamith eagerly consents.

Albrecht proposes to Maria in a chamber of the house where he finds her quietly sewing, but she casts her eyes down and is too shy and modest to respond. Finally, without raising her eyes, she whispers her positive response. Joseph and Elizabeth are delighted. "You, my beloved Sulamith are a pure and noble rose," Joseph says; "you shall make your husband happy through the fruit of your body; you shall lack for nothing; you shall have an abundance of wine and corn. . . . My Maria is a pure and innocent Lily. She will bring delight and contentment to her husband; blessed be the fruit of your love, the child that will play on your bosom. You will have an abundance of wine and corn, and our Savior will mark you out among His elect."

The tale then includes a detailed account of the two young artists' proposals for an altarpiece that the King has commissioned them to paint for the Cathedral, as well as of their plans for two side chapels. Once again Pforr inscribes himself and his friend unequivocally in the story, just as both artists later paint each other along with other *Lukasbrüder* and members of their family, into their history paintings. For one of the chapels – to be known as the chapel of St. John – Johannes designs scenes from the life of St. John the Evangelist; for the other – to be known as the Chapel of Knighthood – Albrecht plans a painting of St. George slaying the Dragon (Pforr in fact produced such a painting **(Pf. 29)**, along with scenes illustrating the knightly virtues. The wedding scene, as Pforr recounts it, is important in that it includes a description of the two brides: Sulamith wears a white dress and a bodice richly decorated with flowers sown in gold; Maria chooses a red dress hemmed in black. She fits Sulamith out with jewels from the latter's jewel box; in particular we are told that she gathers Sulamith's golden hair in a gold clasp studded with rubies and ties a girdle of pure gold studded with diamonds and sapphires around her waist. But Maria herself declines to wear any jewelry other than a small ivory cross with an engraved image of our Lord on it around her neck and two earrings, from which hang tiny pomegranates of beryl. (The red pomegranate customarily symbolizes the wounds of Christ.)

After the wedding, Joseph and Elizabeth set off on a journey from which they return a year later. They find the house of Johannes and Sulamith at the end of a large and beautiful garden full of fig trees, almond trees, vines, and flowers of every description; a clear brook flows through it and young deer, peacocks, and doves wander freely in it. In the handsome, though simple house, before which there is a large palm tree, they find Sulamith with a beautiful little boy on her lap who is only months old. Sulamith shows them through the house and they admire the way it has been decorated with paintings of Old Testament figures: Adam and Eve, the "inspired masters Moses and Aron, the brave knights Joshua and Gideon, the wise kings David and Solomon, the holy prophets and scenes from the books known as the Apocrypha." They visit Johannes's studio, where they see many delicately drawn and painted pictures of New Testament scenes from the life and passion of Christ. Soon they visit the simple house of Maria and Albrecht. In Albrecht's studio they find paintings depicting episodes from the Lives of the Saints and the deeds of the heroes of old. Joseph is content, gives thanks to God, and urges his children to remember the words: "Kindlein liebt euch untereinander" ["Children, love one another"]. As he utters these words "the spirits of all are moved and their hearts are opened to each other in love and harmony."[57]

In Pforr's fable, Sulamith appears as the more open and confident sister. She is more at home in the world and has no difficulty dressing up in fine clothes and jewelry and living in a fine house, even though she remains simple at heart. Maria, in contrast, is modest, retiring, and utterly indifferent to the refinements of everyday life. In Overbeck's drawings, however, as already noted, it is Sulamith (and subsequently Italia) who seems withdrawn and timid, and Maria (later Germania) who is open, confident, and enterprising. In Pforr's "Allegory of Friendship" it was the Sulamith figure who held the hands of the Maria figure while looking directly into her eyes, and in Overbeck's very first sketch **(Fig. XIV, Pf. 30)** it is likewise the Sulamith figure – here on the *right*, identifiable by the hairclasp mentioned in Pforr's fable), but otherwise not yet distinguished by hair color or complexion from her sister figure – who looks directly and confidently at the Maria figure, now with the downcast eyes not untypical of images of the Virgin, on the *left*. In Overbeck's later drawings and in the finished painting, in contrast, it is Maria (now on the *right* and increasingly identifiable by her blond tresses) who takes the hand of the now visibly dark-haired Sulamith (on the *left*) in hers and looks directly and encouragingly at her, while the Raphaelesque figure of Sulamith is passive, withdrawn, and timid, her eyes downcast in what seems as much sadness and resignation as modesty **(Fig. XIII, Pf. 26)**.

A few viewers have commented on this unexpected redistribution of roles in Overbeck's painting and one or two have noted that it is not consonant with the roles attributed to the two figures by Pforr in his fable. "Now Pforr's modest blond-haired (German) bride on the right is the more richly clad and splendid of the two," one scholar writes: "her dress recalls that of Joan of Aragon in the portrait of the latter, attributed at the time to Raphael, in the Doria Pamphili Gallery in Rome. This transformation and this sumptuousness should be seen as a special honor. Maria is now without doubt the more richly adorned and the stronger figure and it is she who is trying with words and gestures of

[57]See the full text ("Das Buch Sulamith und Maria von Franz Pforr") in the rich study of Béla Hassforther, *Das Gemälde "Sulamith und Maria" von Franz Pforr*, M.A. thesis, Kunsthistorisches Institut Heidelberg, 1985 (available on the World Wide Web at www.bela1996.de/art/pforr).

Fig. XIV. Friedrich Overbeck. *Sulamith und Maria.* (1811). Charcoal and black chalk on paper. 47.4 × 56.8 cm. Unsigned. Cambridge, MA, Longfellow House. Courtesy National Park Service, Longfellow National Historical Site.

encouragement to comfort the downcast Sulamith, who seems close to tears."[58] The substitution of a crown of myrtle for the earlier simple crown of oak leaves is another sign, one might add, of Maria's enhanced standing.

Another scholar, an expert on the Nazarenes, also notes the change and offers an explanation of it. According to Frank Büttner, Overbeck at one time defended the right of German art to be itself and not to resemble Italian art. "It is a capital error, that leads to false judgments about German art," he wrote to his father in 1810, "when, without due consideration or understanding of that art's particular, inner characteristics, general demands are made of it that its inner nature makes it impossible for it to satisfy. That is as unfair as expecting oranges to grow on an oak tree." Very soon afterward, however, Büttner goes on, Overbeck concluded that his own path did not lead in the direction of the essentially and characteristically German art that appealed so strongly to Pforr. His task consisted, he now believed, in rediscovering and taking up again the orientation of art under Perugino and Raphael, an orientation abandoned shortly thereafter in Italy itself. Raphael, Büttner argues, now represented for Overbeck the highest perfection of modern art, a universal Christian art transcending all

[58]Gisela Scheffler (as in note 53), p. 13. See also note 56.

differences by embracing everything of value in itself and elevating it – rather as Phidias had represented the highest perfection of universal art for the ancients and the neoclassicists.[59] It seems likely, though Büttner does not say so, that this shift in Overbeck's position coincided with his conversion to Roman Catholicism. Pforr was aware of his friend's views, according to Büttner, and indicated at various times that he felt his own art could not satisfy the requirements set by Overbeck. The latter's Sulamith, he noted in a letter, was a "noble, adorable figure that lies beyond my reach."[60]

In his cartoon of *Sulamith und Maria*, Büttner continues, Overbeck responded to Pforr's feelings of inferiority or inadequacy by generously attributing the active role to Maria. "Maria's body position," he notes, "the look in her eyes, and the movement of her hands define her as the one who is encouraging Sulamith, imparting strength to her, perhaps consoling her." This characterization, he goes on, recalls the ambition that presided over the founding of the *Lukasbund*, namely, that of rescuing art from its current decadence and restoring it to its original dignity and significance. The task of modern German artists, as represented by the *Lukasbrüder*, Overbeck's cartoon implies, was to help art, including Italian art itself, to recover from its exhaustion and to resume its true direction.[61] The subject of Overbeck's famous painting, as Büttner interprets it, is thus, on one level at least, the conversion of art, with Maria (Germany) lovingly encouraging the downcast Sulamith (Italy) and drawing her back to her true artistic vocation: "Kehre wieder, kehre wieder, o Sulamith."

[59]The most important work of Overbeck's maturity, *The Triumph of Religion in the Arts*, gave visual expression to this conviction, as critics like Jacob Burckhardt and Theodor Vischer well understood, when they attacked it as retrograde and out of tune with the actual spirit and experience of the mid-nineteenth century. In the commentary he wrote to accompany the viewing of this work Overbeck declared – perhaps in the spirit of the ideal of *Sympoesie* and *Symphilosophie* developed by the Nazarenes' intellectual mentor Friedrich Schlegel – that in fact Christian art need exclude no "aspect or development of art" and "can embrace them all, but only in order to ennoble and sanctify them" by dedicating them to the service of religion.

[60]Büttner (as in note 8), p. 31.

[61]Büttner (as in note 8), p. 31.

V

It would be appropriate now to consider the name Sulamith, which Overbeck chose for his bride and Pforr took up in his fable. The name is unlisted in most German name-books and appears to have come into use, although still very rarely, only after about 1880. Overbeck's source was therefore uniquely literary and, more specifically, Biblical. Several scholars, beginning with Overbeck's first biographer, Margaret Howitt, have pointed to the appearance of the figure of Sulamith in two odes by Klopstock, a poet revered by Overbeck's father ever since he himself had been a student and aspiring poet at Göttingen. When his beloved young Fritz left Lübeck to study in Vienna, Christian Adolf gave him a copy of the 1771 edition of Klopstock's *Odes* to take along with him.[62] A verse in one of them, the ode entitled "Siona" (1764), runs:

> Liebevoll schauet, o Sulamith
> Siona, mein Blick dir, und freudig nach!
> Es erfüllt Wehmut und Ruh, Wonn' erfüllt
> Mir das Herz, wenn du dein Lied, Himmlische, singst.

["With joy and love, O Sulamith of Zion, my gaze turns toward you. My heart is filled with longing and peace and delight when you, o heavenly one, raise your voice in song."]

The figure of Sulamith that the poet addresses here is usually taken to be his heavenly muse, at once religious and poetic. Inasmuch as Overbeck's female figure can also be viewed as representing religiously inspired art, the artist may well have been moved by the poet to name her Sulamith.

A second passage in Klopstock was actually copied by Overbeck into his diary for October 24, 1811. It is the last verse of the Ode "Aganippe et Phiala," also of 1764. In it Sulamith laments the destruction of the Temple:

> An den Rebenhügeln ergoss die Klage
> Sulamiths sich, Wehmut über dem Graun

[62]Howitt, 1: 197. Brigitte Heise considers Overbeck's choice of the name Sulamith briefly in *Johann Friedrich Overbeck* (as in note 33), pp. 86-92.

Des Tempels in Trümmern, der Stadt
In der Hülle des Entsetzens![63]

["On the vineclad hillsides Sulamith poured out her lament, grief at the horror of the temple in ruins, of the city enveloped in terror."]

Does the apparent sadness of the Sulamith figure in the painting repeat the sadness that fills the heart of Klopstock's Sulamith? And did Overbeck see in Klopstock's sorrowful Old Testament Sulamith, grieving over the ruins of the Temple, a representation of his own grief at the decay of "holy Art"? Or of Synagoga grieving over her humiliation and homelessness? Or possibly of his dismay at the disarray and disunity of Christ's church and at the violence it had suffered at the hands of the armies of Imperial France? (Rome and the Papal States had been occupied in 1808-09 and Pope Pius VII imprisoned.) Perhaps also of his own spiritual condition at a time when he may already have been contemplating his conversion to Roman Catholicism? Is that why the verse struck him so forcefully that he copied it into his diary?

Another possible source for Overbeck's Sulamith figure might be a spiritual emblem book by the prolific Johannes Lassen or Lassenius (1636-1692), containing twenty-six meditations and poems inspired by passages from Holy Scripture. Lassenius's *Verliebte Sulamithin oder Heilige Betrachtungen über Sechs und Zwanzig auserlesene Macht-Sprüche H. Schrifft zur Beförderung der Liebe des gecreutzigten Jesu . . . mit vielen Liebes-Liedern auch erbaulichen Kupffer-Stücken* appeared posthumously in 1698 in Copenhagen, whither the author, a native of Pomerania, had been called by the Pietist Danish king to be the pastor of the German community and where he was soon appointed to a chair at the university. A third edition appeared in 1728. It seems that Lassenius's works were a popular sourcebook for preachers until well into the nineteenth century, copies of them having turned up in many pastors' libraries. As Lübeck lay within the intellectual and spiritual orbit of Denmark, it is reasonable to assume that *Verliebte Sulamithin* was well known there. The great theme of the work, as developed both in the long Introduction, in the individual meditations, and in the hymn-like, baroque verses that conclude each one, is love – God's love of humankind and the human soul's love of and longing for God. As in much Christian and especially Pietist writing, Sulamith, the daughter of Jerusalem, in love with a groom who is identified as Christ (*verliebte Sulamithin*), is the image of the soul. The following verses (2-5) of the erotically charged poem that stands at the end of the third meditation – on Hosea, 2:19 ("And I will betroth thee unto me for ever") – and in which the bride (the *verliebte Sulamithin*) addresses her beloved, can be taken as characteristic of the work as a whole.

[63]*Werke*, 12 vols. (Leipzig: Georg Joachim Göschen, 1798), 1:197.

Komm o Jesu! Meine Zier
  Meines Herzens Lust und Freude
Komm mein Bräutigam zu mir
  Dementwegen Schatz! Ich leide
Tausend Schmerzen, tausend Pein
Ach! Wann kommstu zu mir ein?

Allerschönster Bräutigam
  Der mit mir längst vertrauet
Ach! Mein süsses Gottes Lamm
  Täglich meine Seele schauet
Ob nicht mein so schönes Licht
Durch die dunckle Wolcken bricht.

Eile doch und komm herab
  Meiner Seelen Trost und Zierde
In diss meines Herzens Grab
  Fühlestu nicht die Begierde?
Da mein treues Liebes-Herz
Dich verlangt mit heissem Schmerz.

Es ist meiner Seelen Thür
  Stets mein Herzens Freund dir offen
Tritt einmahl mein Lieb hierfür
  Lass mich doch nicht länger hoffen
Oder wilst du dass ich sterb'
Und aus Ohnmacht ganz verderb.[64]

["Come, sweet Jesus, joy and delight of my heart, come to me, my bridegroom, my treasure. I suffer a thousand torments, a thousand agonies. Oh, when will you come in to me? Fairest groom of all, for so long my betrothed, ah, my sweet Lamb of God, every day my soul searches for a sign that my lovely light might break through the dark clouds. Make haste, then, and come down quickly, jewel and solace of my soul: Do you not sense the desire in this, my heart's deep grave? For my true, loving heart longs for you and suffers cruelly. The door of my soul is always open to you, dear friend of my heart. So please, beloved, enter. Do not have me endlessly hope. Or would you have me grow faint and waste away altogether."]

A further possible, though less likely source that might have added to the connotations of the name Sulamith, is a magazine that bore the name as its title. *Sulamith*, the first Jewish monthly magazine in the German language, began appearing in 1806. It was conceived and edited – by David Frankel and Joseph Wolf – in the spirit of Moses Mendelssohn. The subtitle stated the policy of the journal explicitly: "Eine Zeitschrift zur Beförderung der Kultur

[64]1728 ed. (Copenhagen: Johann Christian Rothen), pp. 123-24.

und Humanität unter der jüdischen Nation" ("A journal for the promotion of culture and humanity among the members of the Jewish nation"). Its goal was to bring well-meaning, educated Christians and Jews together and to prepare the Jews for full integration into German society. In order to achieve that goal, the journal's editors argued, Jews would have to abandon many of their more outlandish local practices, behave more like their Christian neighbors, and share with the latter in the promotion and development of German culture. Most of the articles – biographies, historical sketches, poems, sermons, belletristic and educational pieces – were clearly intended to serve the journal's stated ends. As Overbeck had at least one Jewish friend among the students at the Vienna Academy and as his circle of friends and well-wishers later in Rome included several Jews, including Dorothea Schlegel, the daughter of Moses Mendelssohn, it is possible, though there is no evidence for it, that Overbeck knew of this journal, in which, following a long Jewish tradition, the figure of Sulamith clearly stood for the Jewish people – at a point in its history, in the eyes of the editors, when it was about to find a place in Christian German society. If he did know of it, he might well not have sympathized with the Enlightenment views that inspired it[65] – despite his own father's professed admiration for Mendelssohn ("ein herrlicher Kerl" ["a splendid fellow"][66]). Nevertheless, he may well have been struck by the forceful and traditional use of the name Sulamith.

Finally, on the death of Moses Mendelssohn the *Berlinische Monatschrift* published a "Trauerkantata auf den Tod Moses Mendelssohns," to which the author, the poet Karl Ramler (1725-1798), a friend of Lessing and translator of Horace, gave the title *Sulamith und Eusabia* (i.e., Bathsheba). In it the lover and the mother of Solomon the Wise lament the death of Mendelssohn.[67] To

[65]One of the contributors to *Sulamith*, which ceased publication in 1840, was Mendelssohn's disciple David Friedländer. Writing supposedly on behalf of a number of prominent Jewish families in Berlin, Friedländer had proposed an arrangement by which German Jews would convert on the understanding that they were not required to subscribe to *all* Christian articles of faith and could be exempted from certain rituals and ceremonies (*Sendschreiben an Seine Hochwürden Herrn Oberconsistorialrath und Probst Teller zu Berlin, von einigen Hausvätern Jüdischer Religion* [Berlin, 1799], re-ed. Jerusalem [Hebrew University-Zalman Shazor Center], 1975) – a proposal rejected immediately by Schleiermacher on the grounds that one does not pick and choose among articles of faith. Overbeck, one can be sure, would have subscribed fully to Schleiermacher's position on this point. A later journal, *Jedidja*, also based on a proper name (that given by the prophert Nathan in Samuel 12, 25 to Solomon, the son of David and Bathsheba, and meaning "Beloved of Jahweh"), began appearing in Berlin in 1817. As the title suggests (to Sulamith, the beloved of Solomon, corresponded Jedidja or Solomon, the beloved of Sulamith), it was intended as a pendant to *Sulamith*, but in the spirit of Romanticism placed greater emphasis than the earlier journal on religion. It styled itself "Zeitschrift für Religion, Moral, Pädagogik, Geschichte und orientalische Literatur." (See Friedrich Niewöhner, "Sulamith und Jedidja," in Marianne Awerbuch and Stefi-Jersch-Wenzel eds., *Bild und Selbstbild der Juden Berlins zwischen Aufklärung und Romantik*, [Berlin: Colloquium-Verlag, 1992], pp. 179-209.)

[66]Jansen, *Aus dem Göttinger Hainbund. Overbeck und Sprickmann* (as in note 12), p. 144, letter from C. A. Overbeck to A. M. Sprickmann, 17.4.1777.

[67]See Friedrich Niehwöhner, "Sulamith und Jedidja" (as in note 64).

the degree that the name Sulamith was thus associated with Mendelssohn and his ideas and that Overbeck was aware of this, he could well have imagined, as other Christians had done before him (the most notorious case being that of Lavater), that "Sulamith" and "Solomon" – as "noble Jews" – must logically take the final step and convert, as Dorothea Schlegel had in fact done, and that persuading them to do so was a sincere Christian's duty, since the conversion of the Jews was a crucial moment in the divine plan for the salvation of the world.

Whatever the impact on Overbeck of Klopstock's verses – or, conceivably, of Lassenius's meditations, or even of Frankel's magazine – there is no doubt that, as Pforr's fable itself makes clear, the main source from which the two friends borrowed the name Sulamith was the source that also inspired Klopstock and Lassenius: the Song of Songs or the Song of Solomon, "das Hohe Lied Salomonis" in German. In fact, Overbeck attached a handwritten copy of the Song of Songs to his personal manuscript of Pforr's fable.[68] An assiduous reader of the Bible – a self-portrait of 1809 shows him with an open Bible in his hands **(Pf. 31)** – Overbeck frequently quotes from scripture in his letters and in his diary. A letter of 29 March 1811, describing his *Entry of Christ into Jerusalem* contains several passages from the Song of Songs. A later letter to his mother of the same year (dated 15 September) indicates that he had a special affection for this text and also gives an early sign of his association of the lovely Sulamith with Italy. In this letter he tries to convey his delight at the fruitfulness of nature in Italy: "Only now," he writes, "do I fully comprehend the Song of Songs! Only now does it speak to me so directly! Only now do I understand the sweet yearning that so often came over me when reading it and the pleasure with which I lingered over every image."[69]

Overbeck and Pforr's interest in the Song of Songs was by no means unusual. From earliest times, it had been the most commented-on book in the Bible and had given rise to countless allegorical readings.[70] Only a few decades before Overbeck and Pforr borrowed the name of the bride from it for their own mythology, it had appeared in a completely new translation by Herder (Leipzig, Weygand, 1778). Goethe himself tried his hand at translating it. Herder also wrote a brilliant and spirited Introduction to his translation, in which he

[68]As found in the artist's Nachlass; see Brigitte Heise, "Sulamith und Maria – ein Beispiel romantischer Sympoesie" (as in note 40), p. 41.

[69]Béla Hassforther (as in note 57), p. 44.

[70]Origen, *Commentaire sur le Cantique des Cantiques*, Luc Brésard, Henri Clouzel, Marcel Borret, eds. (Paris: Editions du Cerf, 1991), Introduction, pp. 54, 61. See also Franz Böhmisch, "Exegetische Wurzeln anti-judaistischer Motive in der christlichen Kunst," *Das Münster*, 50 (1997): 345-58, at pp. 348-49; Robert Gordes, *The "Song of Songs" and "Lamentations." A Study, Modern Translation, and Commentary* (New York: KTAV Publishing House, 1954); and especially Arthur Green, "Shekhinah, the Virgin Mary, and the Song of Songs," *AJS Review*, 26 (2002): 1-52.

put forward the modern understanding of the work – this was immediately accepted by Goethe – as a collection of autonomous love poems rather than the single coherent composition that traditional allegorists had used all their ingenuity to discover and interpret.[71] To Herder, the Song of Songs belonged in the same category as other great primitive or, in Schiller's terms, "naïve" poetry, such as that of the ancient Greeks or the newly rediscovered Nordic and Keltic bards (he accompanied his translation with selections from the medieval German *Minnelieder*), and he amused himself and his readers greatly at the expense of theologians, who, from ancient times right down to his own age, had gone to enormous lengths to conceal what to him was the innocent beauty of the Song's literal meaning under a fig leaf of elaborate allegorical readings. Yet Herder's sharpest criticism was reserved not for the allegorizers but for a contemporary orientalist, Johann David Michaelis, who had trivialized the text, in Herder's view, by failing to recognize its poetic character and treating it as if it were a rococo *galanterie*. In contrast, Herder displayed some indulgence toward the allegorists, who at least considered the work seriously and with respect. He even outlined some of their readings, explaining that these did not have to be rejected out of hand, provided they were seen as supplementing the literal meaning instead of shamefacedly repressing it. Allegorical readings of the Song of Songs – and as we saw in our examination of Pforr's painting, the Nazarenes were great allegorizers – were thus readily accessible to Pforr and Overbeck even in the most recent edition of the Biblical text by a much admired modern writer.

Most allegorical readings of the Song of Songs followed a customary pattern of Christian interpretations of Old Testament texts going back to St. Augustine and to St. Paul himself. On the basis of the principle generally referred to, following the Venerable Bede (673-735), as *Concordia Veteris et Novi Testamenti*, Old Testament characters and actions were taken to be allegories or prefigurations of New Testament ones, signs whose full and proper

[71]On Goethe, see *Meine Schatzkammer füllt sich täglich: die Nachlassstücke zu Goethes West-östlichem Divan*, Anke Busse, ed. (Göttingen: Wallstein Verlag, 1999), 2 vols., 1:64; 2:670, 932-33. On Herder, see his *Lieder der Liebe: die ältesten und schönsten aus Morgenlande, nebst vier und vierzig alten Minneliedern* (Leipzig: Weigand, 1778) in *Herders Sämmtliche Werke*, Bernhard Suphan, ed., vol. 8 (Berlin: Weidmann, 1892), pp. 485-680. Also August Werner, *Herder als Theologe* (Berlin: F. Henschel, 1871), pp. 112-15, 220-21, and Rudolf Haym, *Herder* (Berlin: Aufbau Verlag 1954; orig. 1885), 2 vols., 2:106-109. Herder's translation was used for a dramatic production in the early twentieth century: Paul von Klenau, *Sulamith, nach Worten der heiligen Schrift: ein Akt in 6 Bildern* (Vienna/Leipzig: Universal-Edition, n.d.).

meanings were revealed only later by the life of Christ.[72] Within this supercessionist interpretative framework Sulamith was seen variously and often concurrently as a figure of the Christian community, that is to say the Church, *Ecclesia*, as a figure of the individual Christian soul, the lover and beloved of Christ (Origen [early third century] and most prominently Bernard of Clairvaux [1090-1153]), and as a figure of Mary, the mother and at the same time the bride of Christ, herself often a figure of *Ecclesia* (Ambrose [fourth century] and later Rupert de Deutz [1070-1129]). To the degree that Overbeck had the second of those meanings in mind – and, as we saw, the *Sulamithin* served unambiguously in Lassenius's work as a figure of the Christian soul – Maria's reaching out to Sulamith, her apparent attempt to encourage her and reassure her makes sense in terms of the individual Christian's need constantly to renew his or her commitment to Christ and to receive help and support from him and his Church.

In many of the allegorical interpretations Sulamith also signified the Synagogue or the people of Israel. This was, understandably, the common interpretation of rabbinical commentators, who were as eager as their Christian counterparts to read the highly sensual love poems as allegories of spiritual love. In the Jewish tradition, the love of the groom for the bride is God's love for His people, Israel, *kenesset yisra'el*, and the poem is about the steadfastness of this love despite the beloved's infidelities and backslidings. In the Christian

---

[72]On the *Concordia* and typological interpretation, see Friedrich Ohly, "Synagoge et Ecclesia: Typologisches in mittelalterlicher Literatur," in his *Schriften zur mittelalterlichen Bedeutungsforschung* (Darmstadt: Wissenschaftliche Buchgesellschaft, 1977), pp. 312-37; Ohly summarizes the supercessionist view implied by typological interpretations in the spirit of the *Concordia* as "Kontinuität und überlegenheit" ["continuity and superiority"]. Likewise Henri de Lubac, *Méditation sur l'Eglise* (Paris: Desclée de Brower, 1985; orig. 1953), pp. 307-309: "Dans le cadre de l'histoire du salut, en suite de l'Incarnation du Verbe, l'Eglise a pris la suite d'Israel," with the result that there is "sous la discontinuité même, une réelle continuité... un approfondissement... la découverte du sens le plus vrai... l'une des conséquences de la grande 'transposition réelle,' du grand 'passage,' du passage unique et définitif, celui de l'Ancien Testament au Nouveau." It has been noted, however, that allegorical and typological exegesis of the Old Testament was the Church's response to the radical anti-Judaism of Marcion and some other gnostic theologians, who wanted to reject the Old Testament altogether and who denied that the god of the Old Testament was that of the New. In short, it was employed in order to rescue and not simply to diminish the Old Testament. (Franz Bömisch, "Exegetische Wurzeln," [as in note 70], p. 351) See also Wolfgang S. Seiferth, *Synagogue and Church in the Middle Ages: Two Symbols in Art and Literature*, L. Chadeayne and P. Gottwald, trans. (New York: Frederick Ungar Publishing, 1970; orig. Ger., 1964), p. 14 *et passim* and the clear, but critical exposition by Erich Zeuger of three closely related models of the relationship between so-called "Old" and "New" Testaments: the "contrast model," according to which the Old Testament is imperfect and materialist, emphasizing worldly things, whereas the New Testament promises redemption and hope in a kingdom that "is not of this world"; the "relativising model," according to which the Old Testament is the servant of the New, the promise of which the New Testament is the fulfillment, its function being to prepare the revelation of the New Testament; and the "evolutionary model," according to which the Old Testament is the seed and the new Testament the flower. ("Die Bibel Israels – Absage an die Christianisierung des sogenannten Alten Testaments," in *"Räume die Steine hinweg." Beiträge zur Absage an die Judenmission*, Siegfried von Kortzfleisch and Ralf Meister-Karamikes, eds. (Hamburg: E-B Verlag, 1997), pp. 36-77. In the shadow of the Holocaust, many modern Christian thinkers have reconsidered and rejected the supercessionist thesis: e.g., Friedrich Gleis, *Von der Gottesmordlüge zum Völkermord. Von der Feindschaft zur Versöhnung. Kirchlicher Antijudaismus durch zweitausend Jahre und seine Überwindung* (Herb am Neckar: Geiger Verlag, 1995); George Lindbeck, "The Church on Israel: Ecclesiology and Ecumenism," in *Jews and Christians: People of God*, Carl A. Braaten and Robert W. Jenson, eds. (Grand Rapids, Michigan/Cambridge, England: William P. Eerdmanns, 2003); David Novak, "From Supercessionism to Parallelism in Jewish-Christian Dialogue," ibid.; Erich Zeuger (as above).

tradition, beginning with Hippolytus of Rome (early 3rd century) this reading was not erased but, in the spirit of *Concordia*, supplemented and completed. Sulamith thus came to signify sometimes the Synagogue of the Old Covenant and sometimes, as noted previously, *Ecclesia*, the Church of the New Covenant. Many of the commentaries explicitly read Sulamith as the Synagogue and the appeal to her to return in VII,1 as an appeal to the Synagogue to acknowledge the Church as the beloved of Christ, that is, as an appeal to the Jews to convert.

One of the most powerful of such readings is that of the prolific Giles of Rome, who became Bishop of Bourges in 1295. "Christ in this passage," he wrote of 6, 13 ("Return, return, O Shulamite; return, return" ["Kehre wieder, kehre wieder, o Sulamith, kehre wieder, kehre wieder" in the Luther translation of the Bible]), "calls the Synagogue back to him." The passage," he goes on, "may be interpreted as follows: 'since you, Synagogue, or Shulamite maiden, acknowledge the captivity of your misery and blindness, and are aware of your animal nature, *Come back*, by abandoning your mental blindness. *Come back, Shulamite maiden*, by abandoning your animal nature and sensual wickedness. *Come back*, by cleaving to the truth, *so that we may gaze at you*, with a compassionate eye, taking pity on you.' "[73] The Synagogue, Giles declares, "apologizes for her ignorance." At the same time, the celebrated description of the physical beauty of the bride ("your navel is a rounded goblet," etc.) is a commendation by Christ of the Synagogue's continence, perseverance, participation in the active life, and dedication to teaching. The line "I am my beloved's and he is mine" is interpreted as a description of the Synagogue's conversion ("Bekehrung" in German). "First, the Synagogue turns toward him; second, she seeks support and help to do this, where she says, 'Come, my beloved.' " The continuation of this passage – "let us go out into the fields" – is interpreted to mean "Let us go out, that is, to the Jews, who are an untilled field." The passage beginning "Let us go early to the vineyards" evokes the commentary: "She [i.e., the Synagogue] says, 'let us go early,' that is, at the right time. Let us not be lazy, but eagerly and carefully 'let us go early to the vineyards,' that is to the Jews. . . . She asks Christ to come to her help by moving the Jews' hearts." The bride's words "I shall give you my breasts" are to be understood as meaning: "she shows here that the Jews are disposed to receive such help." Moreover, "although we can all call Christ our brother because he assumed humanity, yet the Synagogue in particular can call him brother because he was born of a Jew."[74]

The continuation of the commentary takes the form of an appeal in which the commentator urges the Synagogue to convert and be reconciled with the

[73]Giles of Rome, *Commentary on the Song of Songs and Other Writings*, John E. Rotelle, O.S.A., ed. (Villanova, PA: Augustinian Press, 1998), Lecture 14, p. 147.

[74]Ibid., pp. 158-63.

Church by recognizing and acknowledging the latter as the bride of Christ. Accordingly, the lines "Under the apple tree I raised you up" inspire the following commentary: "In this part the Church is invited to take care of and help the Synagogue, now converted. This part is divided into three: first Christ reminds the Church of the kindness and help he has given her; second in repayment for this he asks for her perpetual love, where he says: place me like a seal; third, for the very love which the Church is bound to have for Christ, he invites her to help the Synagogue, where it is said: 'we have a little sister.' "[75] That line, in turn, receives the commentary: "For the love that the Church must have for Christ, Christ invites her to help the Synagogue, now converted. . . . Whoever loves someone very much must, for love of him, come to the aid of all who have an affinity and connection with him; but you, Church, owe me a great love, as has been shown; therefore you must support the Synagogue which matters to me and is connected to me, for she is my sister. And the greater her need, the more energetic must be your support. And so it will be for the Synagogue at the end of time, for he says: *we have a sister,* by my carnal affinity, by your spiritual affinity, for she is to be gathered into the fold for the same grace. And so you must be moved by affection, because she is connected to me and is to be connected to you. You must also be moved to this by her need, because she is *little*, recently converted, and so needs confirmation." With 8, 10 ("I am a wall and my breasts are like towers"), the process of reconciliation is completed: "The Church's response is given, and this part is divided into two. First in her reply the Church indicates that she is ready and willing to help the Synagogue; second, as a result of this, the Synagogue becomes eager for the Church's love. . . . The Synagogue, seeing the Church's love for her, because for love of God she was prepared to give herself for her confirmation, becomes eager to love the Church. She who before used to call the Church adulterous, degraded, and alienated from God, acknowledges now that she is the true bride of Christ, derived from him and preserved by him." Finally, the lines "You who dwell in the gardens, my friends are listening; let me hear your voice" (8, 13) evoke a vision of the Jews converted and welcomed into the Church. This, according to Giles, is what Christ says: "You, Church, *who dwell in the gardens* in spiritual delight, *my friends*, that is the Jews, who have now become your friends for being my faithful one, are listening, that is, are ready and *waiting for you*, to hear and be taught by you. They show their desire, their heart's wish, saying: Church, *let me*, the Synagogue, united to you by faith and love, *hear your voice*, that is, through preaching." The Church must abandon the sweetness of contemplation for a while, "so that, now that the Jews have been converted and thus

[75]Ibid., p. 167.

have become brothers, she can apply herself to instructing them in morals and doctrine."[76]

The Synagogue also figures prominently in an earlier commentary on the Song of Songs by Williram von Ebersberg (died 1085). Williram's work is notable for its striking format. It is laid out in three columns: the center column gives the text of the Vulgate, the left-hand column a paraphrase in Latin hexameters, and the right-hand column a prose interpretation in a curious mixture of Middle High German and Latin. It was well known, with several editions in the fifteenth and sixteenth centuries and a commentary on it by Junius in 1655. It was republished at Ulm in 1727 and again in 1752 at Augsburg in an edition by David Gottfried Schröber, to whom, as it happens, we also owe an early study of Dürer, *Albrecht Dürer, eines der grössesten Meister und Künstler seiner Zeit Leben, Schaffen und Kunstwerke* (Leipzig: Johann Gottlieb Mauken, 1769). In 1827 yet another edition of Williram appeared at Breslau.[77]

Williram understands the Song of Songs as a dramatic exchange in which the principal actors and speakers are Synagoga, Ecclesia, and Christus (often referred to as "sponsus," the groom). The opening passage, spoken by the dark-complexioned heroine of whom Overbeck may well have been thinking when he described his ideal bride to Pforr (1, 5: "I am black, but comely, O ye daughters of Jerusalem" ["Schwarz bin ich und doch lieblich, Ihr Töchter Jerusalem!" in the Herder translation]), is attributed to Synagoga. But with wonderful assurance, Williram immediately puts the following verses ("My mothers's children were angry with me" ["Die Söhne meiner Mutter zürneten mir"]) in the mouth of Ecclesia and interprets them as follows: "Ich bin primitive Ecclesia. Meine Mutter ist Synagoga. Ihre Kinder judei kämpften so hartnäckig gegen die Christen, dass sie sie aus ihrem Land vertrieben."[78] In general, the emphasis in Williram's reading is on Synagoga's admiration for Ecclesia whom she had formerly despised and attacked, on her acknowledgment that Ecclesia is now the beloved of Christ, and on her willingness to submit to Ecclesia. Thus verse 6, 10 ("Who is she that looketh forth as the morning, fair as the moon, clear as the sun, and terrible as an army with banners") carries the heading "Synagoga de Ecclesia dicit" and is interpreted as follows:

---

[76]Ibid., pp. 172, 174. See Ohly, *Schriften zur mittelalterlichen Bedeutungsforschung* (as in note 72), p. 317: "The passage in the *Song of Songs*, 3: 4 – 'I found him whom my soul loveth: I held him, and would not let him go, until I had brought him into my mother's house' – was understood to refer to Ecclesia, who will convert her mother Synagoga and lead her to Christ before the end of time." Ohly atributes this interpretation to Robert de Tumbalenia, the late 11th century Breton or Norman author of a Commentary on the *Song of Songs*, as well as to Gregory the Great (6th century).

[77]*Williram's Übersetzung und Auslegung des Hohenliedes in doppelten Texten aus den Breslauer und Leidener Handschrift*, H. Hoffmann, ed. (Breslau: Grass, Barth und Comp., 1827). Quotations are from this edition, in which the German has been modernized, and from *Die älteste überlieferung von Willirams Kommentar des Hohen Liedes: Edition-Übersetzung-Glossar*, Rudolf Schützeichel and Brigit Meineke, eds. (Göttingen: Vandenhoek & Ruprecht, 2001). There was a further edition of Williram at Strasbourg in 1878.

[78]"I am the early Ecclesia. Synagoga is my mother. Her children, judei, struggled so obstinately against the Christians that they drove them out of their land."

> Ecclesiam Christi, die ich früher detestabar per ignorantiam, über die kann ich mich jetzt nicht genug wundern, wie erhaben sie ist und wie si immerfort gedeiht de virtute in virtutem. Sie erscheint mir der Aurorae gleich, weil sie post tenebris infidelitatis sich ad verum lumen gewendet hat und erscheint mir so schön wie der Mond. Weil sie sicher weiss, dass sie die pulchritudinem virtutum niemals aus sich selbst hat, sondern durch Gottes Gnade, ebensowenig wie der Mond etwa Licht durch sich selbst hat secundum phisicos, sondern ex illustratione solis. Sie erscheint mir auch erwählt wie die Sonne, weil sie alle ihre Werke nach Gottes Willen gestaltet, qui est sol justitiae, ad cujus contemplationem festinat. Sie erscheint mir auch furchterregend wie die gut angeordnete Zeltreihe, weil sie keine Lücken lässt den malignis spiritibus.[79]

Inevitably verse 6, 13 ("Return, return" ["Kehre wieder"], etc.) is interpreted as Ecclesia encouraging Synagoga to convert ["sich bekehren"]. This conversion of Synagoga is the goal that Christians must strive toward, even though they do not know when it will be realized. The heading Williram gives to the passage is "Ad Synagogam vox consolatoria Ecclesiae" and the interpretation runs as follows:

> O Synagoga, du wunderst dich über die Gnade, die mir widerfahren ist in coruscatione et celeritate evangelii. Dieselbe Gnade ist für dich bereit, si conversa fueris ad redemptorem tuum, den dir lex et prophetae verhiessen, quia lex et prophetae per evangelium adimplentur. Ich weiss das sicher, sobald du conversa fueris, dass einige virtutes an dir sichtbar werden. Das ist für uns erstrebenswert, wenn es immer eher geschehen kann.[80]

Verse 8, 5 ("Who is this that cometh up from the wilderness leaning on her beloved") is again interpreted as expressing the wonderment of Synagoga at the love of Christ for Ecclesia, his Church, and becomes, in addition, an occasion to recall the crucifixion and the earlier bitter hostility of Synagoga, a mother so "corrupta et violata" that she not only did not upbraid those who clamored for Christ to be crucified but accepted responsibility for the crucifixion

[79]"I cannot sufficiently admire how noble the Ecclesia Christi, which I formerly detestabar per ignorantia, now is, how ceaselessly she advances de virtute in virtutem. She seems to me to resemble the Aurora, inasmuch as post tenebris infidelitatis she has turned ad verum lumen and now appears to me as lovely as the moon. Because she surely knows that she does not derive the pulchritudinem virtutum from herself, but only through Divine Grace, just as the moon's light does not come from herself secundum phisicos, but ex illustratione solis. At the same time she seems to me chosen, like the Sun, because she forms all her works according to God's will, which is sol justitiae, ad cujus contemplationem festinat. She also strikes me as awesome, like a well ordered row of tents, because she leaves no empty spaces for the malignis spiritibus."

[80]"O Synagogue, you wonder at the grace that has been granted to me in coruscatione et celeritate evangelii. The same grace can be yours, si conversa fueris ad redemptorem tuum, whose coming was predicted by lex et prorphetae, quia lex et prophetae per evangelium adimplentur. I know for sure that as soon as you conversa fueris some virtutes will immediately be visible in you. If this can be made to happen sooner, that is an end that for us is worth the greatest effort."

even in the name of their children and their children's children. This characteristically hostile presentation of Synagoga is somewhat softened, however, by repeated professions of continuing love and admonitions to convert. Thus 8, 6 ("love is strong as death") is interpreted to mean: Christ urges Synagoga to reflect in her mind and in her heart on his love for her, which was so strong that he suffered death for her sake, and to abandon her fierce hostility to him and to the gentile church (*Ecclesia de gentibus*) and join in union with the latter. "Du sollst ihr saluti congaudere, quia tecum una erit Ecclesia" – "you shall enjoy salvation along with her, because with you, the Church, will become one."

Whether Overbeck and Pforr were familiar with these or similar allegorical readings of the Song of Songs and of the Shulamite figure in the Canticle is unknown, but it seems unlikely that they were not.[81] They were highly cultivated and well-read artists. Overbeck in particular was extremely studious and reflective and had received a thorough classical and religious education. Both traditions are acknowledged in an early self-portrait of 1807 **(Pf. 32)** in which he is portrayed holding both a Bible and a drawing of a classical figure. Literature, philosophy, and theology were part of his background in his father's house in Lübeck. The Senator, diplomat, and later Bürgermeister of the old Hanseatic city was himself a poet of some distinction, a friend of Klopstock, Voss, and Gleim. His letters to his family reveal an urbane, lively, open-minded man of wide interests and curiosities, of consistently liberal and tolerant temper, often witty and playful, yet at the same time a man of quiet religious piety, who, while encouraging his son's artistic bent, also constantly urged on him the importance, for his career as an artist no less than for his personal development, of a broad general culture and of familiarity with the great literary sources of art, both sacred and profane.[82] The Pietist influence in the Overbeck household must also have inclined the young artist toward allegorical and figurative ways of thinking, for although these had faded from contemporary Lutheran orthodoxy, they remained very much alive in Pietist circles.[83] It is almost inconceivable that Overbeck and Pforr, in borrowing from the Song of Songs to create a mythology of their own, were ignorant of the interpretative tradition.

---

[81]For a rich, learned, and stimulating account of both the Jewish and the Christian traditions of interpretation of the Song of Songs, see Arthur Green, "Shekhinah, the Virgin Mary, and the Song of Songs," *AJS Review*, 26 (2002): 1-52.

[82]Gaedertz (as in note 9), p. 78.

[83]Hans-Jürgen Schrader, "Sulamiths verheissene Wiederkehr: Hinweise zu Programm und Praxis der pietistischen Begegnung mit dem Judentum," in *Conditio judaica: Judentum, Antisemitismus und deutschsprachige Literatur vom 18. Jahrhundert bis zum ersten Weltkrieg*, Hans Otto Horch and Horst Denkler, eds., 3 vols., vol. 1 (Tübingen: Max Niemeyer Verlag, 1988), pp. 71-107. "As a matter of principle, [the Pietists] understand every word of the Bible and everything that is said in it about the Jews or that can be taken to refer to them not only as the annunciation of a specific historical situation, but also as a type or figure that is continuously operative in the present, a prefiguring promise of the Holy Spirit with respect to both the total historical plan of divine redemption of the world and the microcosmic sphere of God's dealing with each individual soul" (p. 74).

VI

Conversion ("*Bekehrung*") – a dominant theme, as we have now seen, in many readings of the Song of Songs – was an important personal issue for Overbeck. We noted earlier that the reform of art promoted by the *Lukasbrüder* was not seen by them as a technical matter but required in the first instance the inner spiritual transformation of the artist. Overbeck himself converted to Catholicism, after a long period of self-questioning, on Palm Sunday, 1813, and was subsequently involved in the conversion of several other Protestants and at least one Jew in Rome. The call to Sulamith to return – "*kehre wieder*" – was one that the artist himself had heard and that he wished others to hear. He himself had been Sulamith – the "captive of his wretchedness and blindness," in the words of Giles of Rome. In the early years of the nineteenth century, however, it may have been particularly apt that the figure of the soul being called upon to convert was the dark-complexioned Shulamite, Klopstock's "Sulamith Siona," for in reflection on conversion in the eighteenth and early nineteenth centuries, Jews occupied a prominent place.[84] More and more Jews were in fact converting – not always for opportunistic reasons, as the examples of Moses Mendelssohn's daughters Brendel (later Dorothea

[84]See Michael A. Meyer, *The Origins of the Modern Jew; Jewish Identity and European Culture in Germany 1749-1824* (Detroit: Wayne State University Press, 1967), esp. pp. 87-109; Jacob Katz, *Out of the Ghetto: The Social Background of Jewish Emancipation 1770-1870* (Cambridge, Mass.: Harvard University Press, 1973), pp. 105-121; the article "Converts to Christianity, Modern" in www.JewishEncyclopedia.com. Jewish conversions to Christianity in Berlin grew steadily in number from nineteen in the four-year period 1770-1774 to 381 in the four-year period 1825-1829 according to Steven M. Lowenstein, "Soziale Aspekte der Krise des Berliner Judentums 1700 bis 1830," in *Bild und Selbstbild der Juden Berlins zwischen Aufklärung und Romantik* (as in note 65), pp. 81-105. N. Sammler (*Judentaufen im 19. Jahrhundert* [Berlin: M. Poppelauer, 1906]) and more recently Guido Kisch (*Judentaufen* [Berlin: Colloquium Verlag. 1973]) argue that the vast majority of these conversions were opportunistic, motivated by the desire to enjoy civil rights and win acceptance in German Christian society – and that does appear to be what lay behind David Friedländer's notorious *Sendschreiben an seine hochwürden Herrn Oberconsistorialrath und Probst Teller zu Berlin von einigen Hausvätern jüdischer Religion* of 1799 (see note 65). However, Jacob Katz warns that "it would be a mistake to assume that all those who turned Christian did so with the consciousness, so to speak, of striking a social bargain" (*Out of the Ghetto*, p. 119). This warning is particularly apt in the case of North German Jewish converts to Roman Catholicism – those best known to Overbeck. These converts simply exchanged one form of social disadvantage for another, somewhat lesser one. On nineteenth-century conversions in general, see David August Rosenthal, *Konvertitenbilder aus dem neunzehnten Jahrhundert* (Regensburg. G.J. Manz, 1889; 1st ed. 1865), 3 vols. In vol 1, dedicated to Germany, most of the individuals portrayed are Protestants converted to Catholicism; a small number of Jewish converts is also described.

Schlegel) and Jette (i.e., Henriette) demonstrate.[85] At a time when there was much talk of integrating Jews into the fabric of German society, moreover, many Christians believed conversion of the Jews was a necessary or at least a highly desirable step toward that goal. Above all, for some earnest Christians, as we shall see, the conversion of Jews was a model of all conversion. To Overbeck, "praying for the Jews," as he proposed to do on emerging from the tunnel on the railway line from Milan to Como, may well have had a meaning beyond its literal one: namely, praying not only for his Jewish benefactor, Ascoli, not only for all Jews, but for all, including many who were formally Christians but had no living faith or – like himself for many years – had not acknowledged the one true Church, and were thus in need of illumination and conversion.

The Age of Revolution was also, not surprisingly, an age of radical inner revolutions. The Enlighteners themselves often wrote of their enlightenment in terms of a sudden illumination, similar to a conversion or an effect of divine grace. Descartes describes his discovery of the basic axiom of his philosophy in this way in the *Discours de la Méthode*. In Diderot's *Lettre sur les Aveugles*, a cataract operation serves as a metaphor for enlightenment. In the matter of full civil rights for Jews, Kant and Fichte demanded drastic transformation: To qualify as full-fledged citizens of the modern state, Jews should be required to give up their traditional beliefs and practices – since, according to Kant and Fichte, these did not express any truly religious faith or experience but merely defined an historically produced ethnic or political community.[86] Christians themselves, the two philosophers maintained, closer as they might be to a pure and universal religion than the Jews, needed to free themselves from the positive, historical elements of their faith in order to embrace fully the religion of conscience that was the ideal of the two philosophers.[87] Some revolutionaries – the French Romantic historian Jules Michelet, for one – presented the Revolution itself as a sacred event and the foundation of a new revolutionary religion. Michelet appears to have envisaged his own *Histoire de la Révolution franaise* as the gospel of this new religion, supplanting or completing the sacred books of Christianity as the latter had supplanted and completed those of the Jews.[88]

[85]Still strongly rationalist and unimpressed by Dorothea's conversion to Catholicism in 1808, Henriette herself had a sincere conversion in 1814.

[86]On Kant and Fichte, see Klaus Berghahn, *Grenzen der Toleranz* (Cologne/Weimar/Vienna: Böhlau, 2000), pp. 206-227, especially, pp. 210-211. Berghahn extends his analysis to Humboldt, arguing that despite his consistent advocacy of the emancipation of the Jews, "whenever Humboldt comes to speak of the Jewish religion, he reveals that he is a Christian pragmatist actively promoting the emancipation of the Jews in the apparent expectation of their ultimate conversion." Hence his opposition to reform movements within Judaism. "Assimilation and integration are the aims of Humboldt's policy with respect to the Jews and a reformed and strengthened Judaism would stand in the way of the realization of those aims" (pp. 274, 273).

[87]Berghahn, *Grenzen der Toleranz* (as in note 86), pp. 218, 220.

[88]See "Michelet's Gospel of Revolution," in my *Between History and Literature* (Cambridge, Mass.: Harvard University Press, 1990), pp. 201-224.

In a completely different camp from that of the secular Enlighteners, many serious Christians, rejecting the rationalized and watered-down Christianity of "enlightened" Protestant circles, emphasized the central importance of the inner experience of faith. Pietism in particular sought to bring about the conversion of each individual, by replacing routine, formal observance with living faith. This concern with conversion and inner transformation often led to a considerable preoccupation with the Jews not only as those most in need of conversion and most resistant to it but as exemplary of all who were in need of conversion.[89] At the end of the seventeenth century the founder of the Pietist movement, Philipp Jakob Spener, insisted on the crucial importance of the conversion of the Jews. While acknowledging that in the view of some Christian exegetes the conversion of the Jews, which St. Paul had said would precede the establishment of a single universal Church, had already taken place in the form of the conversions at the time of the Apostles, Spener argued strongly that the conversion of the Jews was still to come and that only then would the final gathering in of all God's faithful in one universal Church occur. He appears to have been uncertain of the role Christians themselves would or should play in that final conversion of the Jews. By turning their own hearts, overcoming the dissent among them through true Christian love, and reforming their community, were they to serve as an example that would lead the Jews to convert, or did Divine Providence have another, as yet unforeseeable plan for converting the Jews and by their example accomplishing the reunification of the community of the faithful? Spener left that question open:

> I do not see how it can be doubted that [by the conversion of the Jews] the whole true Church will be put in a far more blessed and devout condition than it is now. For if the Jews are to be converted, then either the true Church must already be in a holier condition than it is at present, so that its transformation might serve at the same time as a means of achieving the conversion of the Jews, or at least . . . of eliminating obstacles to it; or, if the Jews are to be converted by the power of God in a manner impossible for us to foresee at this point, we surely cannot imagine that the example of such a newly converted people (among whom the same zeal will doubtless be demonstrated as was observed among the earliest Christians when they converted from heathendom) will not bring in its wake a notable change and

[89]"The conversion of the Jews for him [Philipp Jakob Spener, the founder of the Pietist movement] is the model case of the conversion of every human being, as a human being, to God, that is to God as he is revealed in the Bible" (Karl-Heinrich Rengstorf, "Die deutschen Pietisten und ihr Bild des Judentums," in Jakob Katz and Karl-Heinrich Rengstorf, *Begegnungen von Deutschen und Juden in der Geistesgeschichte des 18. Jahrhunderts* [Tübingen: Max Niemeyer, 1994], p. 4); with Johann Heinrich Callenberg, founder of the missionary organization known as the Institutum Judaicum [1728 until 1792] in Halle, "as with Spener, the conversion of the Jews is presented as the exemplary case of the conversion or turning to God – i.e. to the God of Biblical Revelation – of all human beings, not excluding members of the Church" (ibid., p. 11).

> improvement in our Church. Rather it is to be hoped that the single Church constituted by Jews and Gentiles and united by a single faith and the abundant fruit thereof will serve God with unstinting holy zeal.[90]

One thing does seem clear: in whatever manner the conversion of the Jews was achieved, it was central to Spener's entire religious view.

Though some in the Pietist movement believed the Jews should be treated with Christian love ("lieblich und weislich," in Spener's words[91]) as God's chosen people, from whom the Savior had come, but also cautioned that their conversion should be left to Divine Providence, others held that it was a Christian duty to actively proselytize among the Jews and thus, step by step, help to create the conditions for the final fulfilment of history.[92] Even so, eighteenth-century Pietist missionaries had strict instructions not to try to

---

[90]". . . so sihe ich nicht/ wie gezweiffelt werden könne/ daß nicht die gesamte wahre Kirche werde in einem viel seligern und herzlichern stande gesetzt werden/ als sie ist. Dann wo die Juden sollen bekehret werden/ so muß entweder bereits die wahre Kirche in heilgerem stande stehen/ als sie jetzund ist/ daß deroselben heiliger wandel zugleich ein mittel jener bekehrung werde/ auffs wenigste darmit die hindernüß derselben . . . weggeräumet seye: Oder/ wo sie sonsten von Gott durch seine Krafft/ auff uns jetzo noch vorzusehen unmüglich art/ werden bekehret werden/ ist wiederumb nicht zu gedencken, daß nit dz exempel eines solchen neubekehrten volcks (bey dem ohne zweiffel der eiffer sich zeigen wird/ wie bey den ersten auß den Heyden bekehrten Christen zu sehen gewesen/) eine merckliche änderung und besserung bey unserer Kirchen nach sich ziehen solte. Vielmehr ist zu hoffen/ daß mit heiligem eifer gleichsam in die wette die gesamte auß Juden und Heyden versamlete Kirche in einem glauben und dessen reichen früchten GOtt dienen/ und sich an einander erbauen werde" (Philipp Jakob Spener, *Pia Desideria* [1675], in *Schriften*, Erich Beyreuther, ed., 16 vols. [Hildesheim and New York: Georg Olms Verlag, 1979-1989], vol. 1, p. 220 [p. 74 of 1680 ed., reproduced in facsimile]). For the 1678 Latin translation of Spener's *Pia Desideria*, see *Die Werke Philipp Jakob Speners*, Studienausgabe, vol. 1, *Die Grundschriften*, Kurt Aland and Beate Köster, eds. (Giessen and Basel: Brunnen Verlag, 1996), Part 1. p. 175. Spener's tripartite redemptive history recalls that outlined by St. Ambrose in the fourth century: "Umbra praecessit, secuta est imago, erit veritas; umbra in lege, imago in evangelio, veritas in caelestibus" (quoted by Ohly, *Schriften zur Mittelalterlichen Bedeutungsforschung* [as in note 71], p. 324.)

[91]Philipp Jakob Spener, *Schriften*, Erich Beyreuther, ed., vol. 15: *Theologischer Bedencken Dritter Theil* (written 1667-1705, orig. published 1711), "Register der merckwürdigen Sachen,"*sub* "Jude." Under the same heading Spener lists passages where he argues that the Jews – described as "das edelste Volck" ["the noblest of peoples"] – "must be allowed to live and practice their religion among the Christians" and that "preachers must preach seriously and strongly against un-Christian hatred of the Jews." Spener urged, however, that "für sie und ihre Bekehrung ist zu beten" ["we must pray for them and for their conversion"] – precisely the thought that came to Overbeck as he emerged from the tunnel in the anecdote recounted by Hewitt. Spener's admonition never to use violence against the Jews, even in the effort to "save" them, has a long history in Christian thought. Pope Gregory the Great, following St. Augustine's admonitions againt arrogance toward the "broken branch," emphasized that "we never hear of Our Lord Jesus Christ forcing anyone into His service by violent means; on the contrary, He won people over by quiet persuasion; He allowed them to act according to their own free will and brought them out of error not by using threats but by shedding his blood for them." As the modern Christian theologian who quotes this passage acknowledges, Gregory's recommendation fell for the most part on deaf ears. Spener was apparently one of those who took it to heart. (See Karl Thieme, ed., *Kirche und Synagoge: der Barnabasbrief und der Dialog Justins des Märtyrers* [Olten, Switzerland: Verlag Otto Walter, 1945], Afterword, p. 204; also P. Browe, S.J. *Die Judenmission im Mittelalter und die Päpste* [Rome: SALER, 1942].)

[92]Schrader (as in note 83), pp. 87-97. The proselytizing position was still vigorously upheld "eben jetzt bei den Verfolgungen" ["in this very time of persecution of the Jews"], by the theologian Karl Thieme, writing the Afterword to his *Kirche und Synagoge* (as in note 91) on Good Friday, 1944. See Thieme, pp. 217-18.

achieve by force or threat what could only be the work of love and grace.[93] To some Pietists, moreover, as already noted, the conversion of the Jews was a model of conversion in general. They believed that many who called themselves Christians, but whose Christianity consisted of a routine external practice of rites, needed to be converted, as much as any Jew. At the same time, the fate of the Jewish people, their dispersal and humiliation, was seen as a figure or model of the fate of *Ecclesia*, the Christian community.[94] The conversion of the Jews would thus signify at the same time the recovery of the lost unity of Christ's Church. In this way the conversion of the Jews served both as a model of the transformation of the individual soul and as a condition of the fulfilment of the divine plan for mankind as a whole.

By the late eighteenth century the Pietist movement had been taken over to a considerable degree by the orthodox Evangelical and Reform churches. But it is not unlikely that one aspect of the original impetus behind it – an ardent, at times Chiliastic longing for the overcoming of divisions among the various established Churches and for the coming of God's kingdom on earth, "das letzte Reich" – underlay some of the striking conversions from Protestantism to Catholicism that mark the end of the eighteenth century and the early Romantic period. An essentially ecumenical movement, Pietism consistently tried to avoid becoming yet another sect, seeking instead to turn the hearts of all, including the Jews, to the God of Biblical Revelation.[95] It might not be accidental that Count Leopold zu Stolberg, perhaps the most famous convert to Catholicism of the late Enlightenment and early Romantic period, came from a family background characterized "in comparison with Orthodox Luther-

---

[93]Callenberg scrupulously avoided describing the theology students he encouraged to work among the Jews as "missionaries." He referred to them as "Mitarbeiter" ["collaborators"]. In their external appearance, moreover, they looked like itinerant artisans and, as they were not ordained, they could not perform baptisms. "Their task was not to win recruits for the Evangelical Church but, as they themselves put it, to move hearts in such a way that they would turn toward Jesus as Savior. In this sense, Callenberg did not wish to bring about the dissolution of Judaism by getting Jews into the Church. His aim was to assist Jews to come to a determination of their own, as he himself had done, thanks to Spener and Francke" (Rengstorf [as in note 88], p. 7). The emphasis, Karl-Heinrich Rengstor insists, was on "liebevolle Zuwendung" ["loving care"]. "Neither in Callenberg's case nor in that of Schultz [Stephan Schultz, 1714-1776, his successor] is there any indication of Christian arrogance toward the Jews. . . . On the contrary, an attitude of love and responsibility on the part of Christians is called for" (Rengstorf, p. 10). The chief effort of the "Mitarbeiter" was to get the Jews to return to the Bible, from which modern Judaism, in the eyes of the Pietists, had strayed far. "If it were ever to come to a new rapprochement and even a community of Jews and Christians, both of whom, after all, have their roots in Biblical revelation, the Jews, like everyone else, would need to turn back to the Bible as the Word of God" (Rengstorf, p. 11).

[94]See Schrader (as in note 83), pp. 72, 78. In general, Schrader sees the Pietists' tendency to allegorize as closely related to their attitude to the Jews; see note 83 above. See also, Peter Schicketanz, *Der Pietismus von 1675 bis 1800* (Leipzig: Evangelische Verlagsanstalt, 2001), p. 129, on Zinzendorf and the notion of "Tropos" – the idea that "Glaubenslehren sich in verschiedenen Erziehungsweisen geschichtlich entwickelt haben."

[95]What the Pietists hoped to repair, according to Schrader, was the "break-up of Christendom into different confessions," what they looked forward to was a "future philadelphian commmunity, a community of brotherly love, constituted by 'awakened' members from *all* churches" (p. 72). On the eschatological, Chiliastic strain in Pietism, see Gerhard Kaiser, *Pietismus und Patriotismus* (Frankfurt a. M.: Athenäum Verlag, 1973), pp. 49-53.

anism, by the irenic and ecumenical spirit of Herrenhut."[96] Or that he had been so struck by a Utopian plan of Overbeck Senior to establish a new community on principles of Christian love and justice on the island of Tahiti – a plan drawn up with seemingly quite serious intent in response to a proposal by Overbeck's friend Sprickmann that the two of them emigrate to America and seek freedom in the New World – that he wrote it up as a Utopian novel.[97] It is not difficult to imagine that this Pietist longing for unity and universality was transferred to the Church that still claimed to be the universal Church, the Church that stood and continued to stand before and above all the divisions of the Reformation. This may in fact be a more plausible explanation of the attraction of Catholicism for many earnest young poets and artists than the supposed esthetically seductive aspects of Catholic ritual – the reason usually adduced by Protestants critical of these conversions. In the early years of the nineteenth century, such conversions from Protestantism to Catholicism were certainly far from uncommon, especially after the widely publicized conversion, in 1800, of Stolberg. Those who, like Stolberg or Friedrich Schlegel, converted to the universal Catholic Church as the authentic guardian of truth, knowledge, and morality, were no defenders of a worldly institution that they knew had been in some measure contaminated by the vices of the ancien regime. The ideal of these enemies of baroque sensuousness was the early Church, simple, austere, undivided, and focused on salvation rather than on power or worldly splendor. This early, universal Church, they believed, lived on in the ancient Church of Rome, despite the latter's shortcomings.[98] Thus in the circle of Friedrich and Dorothea Schlegel there appears to have been much sympathy

---

[96]Peter Noss in *Biogaphisch-Bibliographisches Kirchenlexikon*, vol. 10 (1995) columns 1527-1550, col. 1527.

[97]See Heinz Jansen, *Aus dem Göttinger Hainbund* (as in note 12), pp. 90-97. As written up by Stolberg in the utopian novel *Die Insel* (Leipzig: Georg Göschen, 1788), Overbeck's plan had the character of an agrarian community based on simplified Christian principles. It was, in the view of one scholar, like most Utopian projects, at once a critique of the rationalist and absolutist view that the social order is and should be upheld by the power of the state and a confession of practical powerlessness to effect any real change in the social order; see Dirk Hempel, *Friedrich Leopold Graf zu Stolberg (1750-1819): Staatsmann und politischer Schriftsteller* (Weimar/Cologne/Vienna: Böhlau, 1997), pp. 143-48.

[98]Defending herself in a letter to her friend Karoline Paulus, the wife of a well-known Protestant theologian, against the charge of having yielded to the Catholic mania of the times (Karoline was later to refer disdainfully to the Schlegels as "neupoetische Katholiken"), Dorothea Schlegel insisted that genuine Catholics were as far removed from modish ones as the "insipid chatter that issues from our Protestant pulpits" ["fades Geschwätz, das uns von unseren protestantischen Kanzeln ertönt"] was removed from the true spirit of Luther (letter of 1.12.1805, in *Briefe von Dorothea und Friedrich Schlegel an die Familie Paulus,* Rudolf Unger, ed. [Berlin: B. Behr's Verlag, 1913], pp. xvii, 73-74, 78). As for Friedrich, Dorothea added, creating a new religion was the last thing on his mind. "Eine *neue* Religion hätte Friedrich stiften wollen, meinst Du? Das kann er nicht gewollt haben, man macht keine neue Religion. Hat er von Religion gesprochen und von Poesie, so war es gewiss immer *die Alte, und zwar die alterälteste, die Uralte; die vor Alter vergessene und deswegen für die ganze Welt wieder Neue*" (italics added). ["You think that Friedrich wanted to found a *new* religion? He cannot possibly have wanted anything of the sort. One does not make new religions. If he spoke about religion and poetry, it was certainly always about *the Old Religion and indeed the oldest of the old, the utterly Ancient Religion, which is so old that it has been forgotten and thus seems New again to everybody.*"] She admits that "der moderne Katholizismus ist nicht mehr der ursprüngliche" ["modern Catholicism is no longer the original Catholicism"]. But if poetry is ever to bloom again, it will have to be on the soil of a renewed Catholicism, that is, of the rediscovered "alterälteste, uralte" religion.

in the 1830s for the ideas of Lamennais, Lacordaire, and Montalembert.[99] Moreover, Schlegel's notion of the real revolution – "die grosse, ernste, Gottes-Revolution" ["the great, serious Divine Revolution"] – which the time, according to him, truly demands, now that the "kleine, kindische Menschen-Revolution vorbei ist" ["small, childish Human Revolution has come and gone"][100] – has something of the old longing for final redemption about it. Like many Pietists in the previous century, Friedrich Schlegel may well have thought of the emancipation and conversion of the Jews as the prelude to the Kingdom of God.

Conversion was thus both an important issue in early-nineteenth-century Germany and a matter of central concern to Overbeck personally, as an artist and as a human being. It continued to play a key role throughout his life.[101] He is generally held to have been chiefly responsible for Wilhelm Schadow's conversion in 1814 (Schadow's mother was herself a convert from Judaism), and in the 1830s he was instrumental in bringing about the conversion of Emilie Linder, a talented woman painter and generous patron of art from Basel, who had settled in Rome. It is characteristic of his earnest temperament that conversion for Overbeck was no more a simple matter of recruiting into the Roman Church than the conversion of the *Lukasbrüder*, as artists, had been a mere matter of changing artistic technique.[102] What counted was the process of conversion itself: serious reflection on the most important questions in life and, with divine help, transformation of the individual soul. In contrast to the poet Clemens Brentano, whose insistence – intensified by mystical eroticism – had the effect of making Emilie Linder hesitate about converting, Overbeck advised her not to let herself be pressured but to seek her own way patiently and sincerely, trusting in God to lead her where and when he wanted. In the case of another German artist, the Hamburg painter Friedrich Wasmann, who was in Rome in the early 1830s and who had already converted to Catholicism, Overbeck saw his task as that of giving the young man's conversion – which, by Wasmann's own account, had been a formal affair – a seriousness and

[99]Letter from Dorothea Schlegel to Sophie Schlosser, Frankfurt, 5.7.1834, in Josef Körner, ed. *Krisenjahre der Frühromantik*, vol. 2 (Brno/ Vienna/ Leipzig: Rudolf M. Rohrer, 1937), pp. 490-91. Dorothea apparently was sent copies of the writings of Lamennais and Lacordaire by the authors themselves.

[100]*Kritische Friedrich Schlegel Ausgabe*, Ernst Behler, ed., 35 vols. (Munich: Schöningh, 1958 in progress), 22 (1979): viii.

[101]See Andreas Blühm, "'Herr vergieb ihnen, sie wissen nicht was sie thun.' Overbeck und seine Kritiker," in *Johann Friedrich Overbeck 1789-1869. Zur zweihundertsten Wiederkehr seines Geburtstags*, Andreas Blühm and Gerhard Gerkens, eds. (Exhibition Catalogue, Lübeck Behnhaus, 25.6. – 3.9.1989), pp. 63-79. Blühm contrasts Overbeck's forbearance toward critics and seeming indifference to criticisms of his art with his zeal in the matter of conversions: "Overbeck's missionary zeal was virtually unrestrained. He struggled hard, without success, to bring Schnorr and Speckter into the Catholic fold. He believed he had come closer to his goal in 1833 with Paul Chenavard [the French painter]. Whether in personal encounters or in letters, whether with relatives or with friends, with Protestants or with Jews, Overbeck's efforts at conversion cover his entire life span from the time of his own conversion in 1813" (p. 70).

[102]The Pietists had already roundly condemned proselytizing among the Jews as a means of increasing the strength of the proselytizing churches (Schrader [as in note 83], pp. 101-103).

spiritual content that it did not yet have. The same earnestness is evident in his attitude to Wasmann's practice of art, which at the time was more realist and also more painterly than that of most of the Nazarenes. Each individual, he held, had to find his own way to a spiritually infused, "true" art. It was not a matter of mechanically copying models. "It cannot be my wish to persuade you to adopt another way of practicing your art," he told Wasmann. "The question is not whether one paints images of saints or not. Every artist carries throughout his life a single image within himself, which it is his mission to paint – the image of God that we carry in our soul. . . . Whoever succeeds in executing that image in such a way that it resembles its heavenly model will be accounted a good painter in the eyes of God and His angels, even though his actual material work, painted in colors on wood or canvas, is judged by connoisseurs and laymen to be worthless, good only for being cast into the flames. In contrast, whoever does not execute this one image to the satisfaction of Him who commissioned it will be . . . an object of scorn and contempt in the eyes of the angels, even though generations of viewers on earth praise his work to the skies."[103]

In the circles in which Overbeck moved in Rome and among his fellow-artists, conversion had become frequent enough to be a cause of concern to the Prussian authorities. Inasmuch as being a patriotic Prussian was often seen as equivalent to being a good Protestant (hence the usual pattern of Jewish conversions to Christianity), conversion to Catholicism could be viewed as a politically subversive act. Some nineteen German artists converted to Catholicism in Rome in the early years of the Nazarene movement, according to one source, and that number included several prominent friends and associates of Overbeck's, such as the art historian and critic Carl Friedrich von Rumohr, the Riepenhausen brothers, and the the two sons of Gottfried Schadow, who had designed the Quadriga atop the Brandenburg Gate in Berlin – the painter Wilhelm Schadow, and his younger brother, the neoclassical sculptor Rudolf

[103]Howitt, 2:49. Wasmann's own account of Overbeck's role in his inner conversion, given orally to Howitt, is in Howitt, 2: 44–47. Similar sentiments in some early verses (with an interesting circular rhyme pattern), which Philipp Veit addressed to his friend, the poet Joseph von Eichendorff, in response to the latter's "An Philipp Veit":

> So lass uns fest am Ewigen denn halten,
> Zur Liebe Christi unsern Sinn gewöhnen,
> Der uns zuerst mit ew'ger Liebe bindet.
>
> So wird, was spurlos hier vielleicht verschwindet,
> Was wir gewollt in Farben oder Tönen,
> Am Thron des Herrn zum Ew'gen sich gestalten.

["Let us then hold fast to what is eternal, focus our minds on the love of Christ, who binds us to Him with ties of eternal love. Then that which we desired to achieve in color or in sound and which here may vanish without trace will turn, before the throne of the Lord, into something eternal."]

(*Dorothea von Schlegel geb. Mendelssohn und deren Johannes und Philipp Veit: Briefwechsel* [as in note 25], 2:453).

or Ridolfo Schadow. "Almost everyone who goes to Rome, comes back a Catholic," Ernestine Voss, the wife of the neoclassical poet and a close friend of the Overbecks, complained to the artist's father shortly before the latter was himself obliged to swallow "the heavy, indigestible morsel," as he put it, of his own son's conversion.[104] The "epidemic" of conversions alarmed not only artists faithful to Protestantism, like the painter Louise Seidler,[105] but the Prussian ambassador, Barthold Georg Niebuhr, the celebrated historian of ancient Rome. Niebuhr, who appears to have had an equally strong dislike of Jews and Catholic priests, declared that, though converting might have done some people good (it had turned Wilhelm Schadow, for instance "from a weak and licentious youth into an honorable and virtuous man"), the Catholic Church itself was corrupt[106] and the Roman priests and prelates were "ein Scheisspöbel."[107] "Anyone here who isn't strengthened in his Protestantism to the point of rage [against the Catholic Church]," Niebuhr pronounced, "must be a miserable weakling. Even our German Catholics feel that way."[108] Although he refrains from condemning several young artists who converted to Catholicism on the grounds that "they knew not what they were doing" ["Sie haben nicht gewusst, was sie taten"] and claims to have nothing against those born into the Catholic faith (in fact, his favorite among all the artists was the Catholic Peter Cornelius, a strong German patriot), he complained bitterly that the conversions were creating dissension in the local German community.[109] Niebuhr told his friend, the great legal scholar Friedrich Karl von Savigny, that Overbeck had stopped visiting him – a result, Niebuhr assumed, of the artist's "religiöse Verkehrtheit" ["religious derangement"] and the baleful influence on him of the brothers Johannes and Philipp Veit, who, as Jewish converts to Catholicism, must have been doubly diabolical from Niebuhr's point of view.[110] "This likeable young man has unfortunately fallen so much into the hands of the priests that he has been completely bewitched and infantilized by them as well as by others whom one can only look on as evil priests (the Veit brothers, for example)."[111]

In response to the wave of conversions, Niebuhr arranged for his First Secretary, Christian Bunsen, to organize a celebration of the 300th anniversary

[104]Gaedertz (as in note 10), pp. 84-85; see also Friedrich Noack, *Deutsches Leben in Rome 1700 bis 1900* (Stuttgart and Berlin: J.G. Cotta'sche Buchhandlung Nachfolger, 1907), p. 161.

[105]Though a close friend of Dorothea Schlegel and her son Philipp Veit, both ardent Catholic converts, Seidler expressed dismay at the large number of German artists converting to Catholicism, praised those who resisted the blandishments of ingratiating priests, and admired Niebuhr for his efforts to bolster the Protestant community by persuading the Pope to permit the establishment of a Lutheran place of worship in Rome. *Erinnerungen und Leben der Malerin Louise Seidler* (as in note 25), pp. 255-64.

[106]Barthold Georg Niehbuhr, *Briefe: Neue Folge 1816-1830*, Eduard Vischer, ed., 4 vols. (Bern and Munich: Francke Verlag, 1982-1984), 1: 316-18, letter 125, to Savigny, 20.6.1818.

[107]Ibid., 1: 116, letter 19, to Savigny, 21.12.1816.

[108]Ibid.

[109]Ibid., 1: 316-18, letter 125, to Savigny, 20.6.1818.

[110]Ibid., 1: 259-60, letter 87, to Savigny, 26.12.1817.

[111]Ibid., 1: 241, letter 82, to G.A. Reimer, his Berlin publisher, 29.11.1817.

of the Reformation, to which all German artists in Rome were invited, at his residence, the Palazzo Astalli, on 2 November, 1817.[112] The Catholic contingent, led by the Catholic converts, responded to what they took to be a provocation with a pamphlet – *Ruf der Kirche an die Protestanten* – in the drafting of which Dorothea Schlegel's son, Philipp Veit, played a significant role. This rekindled the ire of Niebuhr and aggravated the divisions in the German artists' colony. Even Jacob Salomon-Bartholdy, the Prussian Consul-General to the Italian States, a converted Jew whom Niebuhr considered a rival and arch-enemy and unfailingly referred to as "der Jude Bartholdy" ["the Jew Bartholdy"] or "der getaufte Jude und Hofrath Bartholdy" ["the baptized Jew and Court yCounselor Bartholdy"],[113] but who had been an important early patron of the *Lukasbrüder* and the Nazarenes, may have fallen out with his nephews, Philipp and Johannes Veit, both closely associated with the new artistic movement, over their fervent Catholicism.[114] Bartholdy himself, like his nephew and niece, the musical prodigies Felix and Fanny Mendelssohn-Bartholdy, had been baptized (in1805) in the official Prussian religion of state and, as a patriotic Prussian and devoted servant of the state, had in all likelihood no more patience than Niebuhr with conversions to Catholicism. What is certain is that only four years after awarding them their first major commission, he turned against his former protégés, writing a scathing anonymous review in the *Allgemeine Zeitung* for 23 July 1819 of an exhibition they had mounted in Rome earlier that year in order to showcase their work and attract much-needed commissions. Barely concealing his anti-Catholicism, Bartholdy anticipated later criticisms of the Nazarenes from Theodor Vischer and Jacob Burckhardt by deploring the "life-

[112]Noack, *Deutsches Leben in Rome* (as in note 104), p. 162.

[113]E.g. Niebuhr, *Briefe: Neue Folge* (as in note 105), 1: 205, letter 60, to the Crown Prince of Prussia, 12.7.1817; 1: 210, letter 65, to Reimer, 14.8.1817; 1: 397, letter 157, to the Crown Prince of Prussia, 26.9.1818. Niebuhr's fear that Bartholdy was angling to replace him surfaces in many letters (e.g., *Briefe: Neue Folge*, 1: 344, letter 137, to Nicolovius, 19.8.1818, and 1: 375, letter 145, to Nicolovius, 11.9.1818). He expresses his intense dislike of Bartholdy openly in letters to various correspondents (e.g., letter 156, to Eichhorn, 26.9.2828, *Briefe*, 1: 391). He may also have resented Bartholdy's influence on the artists, lamenting that because of the neglect of them by the authorities in Berlin, "it fell to a Jew to submit a proposal for promoting this branch also of our nation's industry" (*Briefe: Neue Folge*, 1: 235, letter 78, to Stein [who, unlike Hardenberg, was not well disposed toward Jews], 15.11.1817). Equally he was angered by what he took to be the influence of Bartholdy's later criticism of the Nazarenes on the Prussian decision to reject the conditions Cornelius had attached to his accepting a position in Berlin – which led to the artist's taking up a position in Munich instead. Cornelius, he wrote to the Crown Prince of Prussia was "a Goethe among artists" and it was deplorable that Prussia had lost his services as a result of his having been "persecuted by the anger – not of a Jupiter – but of a contemptible little Jew" (*Briefe: Neue Folge*, 1: 474, letter 216, 25.9.1819).

[114]Veit never gave up his commitment to a Catholic art. His teaching at the art school attached to the prestigious Städelsches Kunstinstitut in Frankfurt am Main, of which he had been appointed Director in 1829, emphasized a Christian and more particularly Catholic orientation toward art (Edward von Steinle and Moritz von Schwind were among the students he attracted), and in the spirit of Overbeck he created a large fresco – *Die Einführung der Künste in Deutschland durch das Christentum* – for the Institute's museum. He also tried to exercise control over the Institute's acquisition policy in the same Catholic spirit. This led him in 1843 to oppose the projected acquisitionl by the Städel of Carl Friedrich Lessing's *Johannes Huss vor dem Konzil zu Konstanz*. The board of the Städel held its ground, leading Veit to resign as Director.

lessness" of their work.[115] (The fact that Niebuhr had encouraged the Nazarenes to organize this exhibition may also have had something to do with the harshness of Bartholdy's review of it; Bartholdy cannot have been unaware of Niebuhr's bad mouthing of him.) Even Dorothea Schlegel's intimate friend Henriette Herz, the celebrated Berlin *salonnière* – "Tante Herz" to the two Veit boys, to whom she was utterly devoted – expressed misgivings about the ardent Catholicism of many young German artists in Rome. Noting that German art was at a turning point during her sojourn in Rome (1817-1819) and that the new orientation of the young artists she frequented there was "eine ernste und würdige" ["an earnest and worthy one"], marked by rejection of the wordliness and banality of the art of their elders, Herz added that it was nonetheless to some degree "one-sided" and intolerant. Anyone harboring other ideas about art kept quiet about them, she claimed, "aus Furcht Anstoss zu geben" ["for fear of giving offence"], with the result that the Nazarene style was becoming entrenched and increasingly mannered. The reason, according to her, was that "that particular view of art had something of the fanatical about it, for it was closely connected with the religious beliefs of the artists, most of whom were recent converts and thus all the more passionate." This religious zeal, Herz

[115]The review is dated Rome, May 1819. Though it appeared anonymously, it was generally known in Rome that Bartholdy was the author. Although some of their criticisms of baroque and rococo painting were justified, Bartholdy conceded, the Nazarenes' work lacked a character of its own ["eigenthümliches Gepräge"], with the result that "one often cannot tell whether one is looking at a nineteenth-century original or a copy of a work from the fourteenth century." He objected, in addition, to a flatness ["eine Flachheit"] that affects even the portraits, so that they "bear the stamp of a certain artistic manner more than they convey the character of the subject being portrayed." In general, Bartholdy notes (correctly, but disapprovingly) that in the work of the Nazarenes "spatial perspective is disdained, and background and foreground elements are executed with the same industriousness, so that, as in certain tapestries, all objects appear very close to the viewer, in the same plane, and without any relief, thanks to their sharp contours, which seem to have been scratched in with an iron stylus." In addition, "the fleshtones – admittedly the hardest thing in the practice of art – are the most imperfect thing about these works. No blood flows through this flesh. One looks in vain for the life and warmth of the Venetians, the boldness and freshness of a Rubens. There is seldom any sign of the artists' having studied Titian or Paolo Veronese; even more rarely has anything been learned from Correggio and Rembrandt, the masters of chiaroscuro" (*Beilage zur Allgemeinen Zeitung*, 23 Juli 1819, No. 124, pp. 493-496, at p. 494, col. 1 and 2, and p. 495, col. 2). Bartholdy's comments were taken up again later by Vischer, Heine, Burckhardt, and many others who had little interest in or sympathy for what the Nazarenes were trying to achieve through their renunciation of modern painterly technique. Even the sympathetic J. Beavington Atkinson regretted that "Venetian splendours are eschewed in favour of pigments thin, dull, and crude" and recalled that "a picture is different from a homily; that art has to be valued for her own sake, that drawing, composition, light, shade and colour are indispensable elements in every art work." Overbeck, he concluded, "shirks the stern truth that the first duty of a painter is to paint" (J. Beavington Atkinson, *Overbeck* [as in note 20], pp. 68-69). Atkinson attributed "the infirmities of Overbeck and his school" to what he deemed their subordination of painting to ideas and, in particular to Overbeck's decision to "embody in pictorial form his friend's [i.e. Friedrich Schlegel's] teachings." This led him to "forget that the most holy of motives cannot save a picture which is not good as a picture" (pp. 38-39).

held, threw a shadow over the relations between many German artists and their Protestant countrymen, artists and nonartists alike.[116]

Among the people close to Overbeck in Rome and active in support of the *Lukasbrüder* and their ideals Jewish converts were prominent. Moses Mendelssohn's daughter Dorothea Schlegel **(Pf. 33)** was an early and ardent champion of the young painters. Since her separation from her first husband, the Berlin banker Simon Veit, her marriage to Schlegel, and her conversion, first to Protestantism and then, along with Schlegel, whom she encouraged to take the step,[117] to Catholicism, Dorothea had become a committed and devout Christian. Living in Vienna, but as yet unacquainted with the young art students who at that very time were banding together at the Academy, she already sympathized thoroughly with their goal of placing art once again in the service of "truth" – that is, Christianity – and making it an instrument of public edification, rather than a private pleasure of the rich and powerful. The function of art, she wrote in 1808 to her two sons, Philipp and Johannes (Jonas, before his conversion in 1810), both art students in Dresden at the time, should be to glorify religion. "Art ought to flow back to the source from which all art springs – that is to say, to God. Every other use of it, for the passing vanities of the human body and human life, is unholy and unworthy of its divine origin. Music and painting, architecture and noble drapery should express only one single idea and should be not the egoistic possession of one individual but the common property of all for the purpose of awakening reverence in all believers."[118] "There is no art of painting," she added a couple of months later, "without Christianity. Whoever is without faith, hope, and charity, for that person nature is only a wilderness in which he sees nothing but himself, and art, likewise,

---

[116]". . . Jene Kunstaussicht etwas von Fanatismus an sich trug, denn sie hing mit dem religiösen Bekentnisse der Künstler zusammen, welche noch dazu meist Neubekehrte, und daher im Glauben um so eifriger waren" (From Henriette Herz's *Tagebücher* or diaries, in *Henriette Herz. Ihr Leben und ihre Erinnerungen*, I. Fürst, ed. [Berlin: Verlag von Wilhelm Hertz, 1850], pp. 220-221). Bartholdy also deplored the "Fanatismus für ihr System" that the Nazarenes had shrewdly kept more to themselves ["im Busen verschliessen"] as long as they were still few in number, and which had, in his view, led to mannerism (*Beilage zur Allgemeinen Zeitung*, 23.7.1819, p. 494, col. 1). As Herz was friendly with Bartholdy (both came from the top layer of wealthy Berlin Jewish families), she may well have been echoing judgments that she had either heard him express directly or had read in his review in the supplement to the *Allgemeine Zeitung*.

[117]See her letter to Friedrich, dated Cologne, 1806, in *Dorothea v. Schlegel geb. Mendelssohn und deren Söhne Johannes und Philipp Veit: Briefwechsel* (as in note 25), 2 vols., 1: 196. Dorothea urges her husband not to procrastinate, not to pursue endless questions, and while properly taking account of his mother's likely reaction to his conversion, not to allow that to stand in his way, since in any case he cannot be sure exactly what her reaction will be. "The whole world knows that in spirit you have long been Catholic." ["Dass Du dem Geiste nach längst katholisch bist, dass weiss die ganze Welt."]

[118]"Da, wo alle Kunst herkommt, von Gott, soll sie auch wieder zurückströmen; jeder andre Gebrauch, zu vorübergehender Eitelkeit der Menschen-Leiber und Leben, ist unheilig und des göttlichen Ursprungs nicht würdig. Musik und Malerei, Baukunst und edle Gewänder sollen nur *eine* Idee aussprechen und nicht das selbstische Eigentum *eines*, sondern ein ganz allgemeines Gut zur Erweckung der Andacht aller Gläubigen werden" (*Dorothea v. Schlegel geb. Mendelssohn und deren Söhne Johannes und Philipp Veit: Briefwechsel* [as in note 25], I: 317, letter to her sons in Dresden, from Vienna, 10.12.1808).

only a vain reflection of his own arrogant imaginings."[119] To Sulpiz Boisserée, the famous collector of early German art, with whom she had become friendly when she and Friedrich Schlegel took the two Boisserée brothers in as boarders in 1803, during their stay in Paris, she wrote expressing her hope for "eine Wiederbelebung der Kunst" ["a revival of art"].[120] Like the future Nazarenes, she did not expect it to come from the art academies. Instruction in painting at the Vienna Academy is not up to much, she wrote her sons: "Füger [the Director] lebt en grand seigneur und kummert sich um nichts" ["Füger lives in grand style and is unconcerned with anything"].[121] In 1810, the year in which the *Lukasbrüder*, as yet unknown to either her or her sons, turned their backs on the Vienna Academy and set out for Rome, she told Sulpiz Boisserée that Philipp would not stay in Vienna because "as far as art is concerned, Vienna has very little to offer" ["für die Kunst ist in Wien gar wenig zu holen"].[122] By the following year, having been informed of Overbeck's ideas about art by Johannes, who had met the artist in Rome and immediately become an enthusiastic admirer and follower, she and Friedrich were already urging Overbeck to send samples of his work to Vienna so that as many people as possible might learn of it. As President of the Vienna Academy, Metternich might be able to arrange for samples to be shipped from Rome to Vienna, Friedrich Schlegel suggested, but immediately corrected himself as he reflected that "die Freunde" that is, the *Lukasbrüder* – "mit den alten Perücken der Akademie nicht zum besten stehen mögen" ["may not be on the best of terms with the old stuffed-shirts at the Academy"].[123]

Philipp and Johannes were in fact both drawn into the circle of the Nazarenes at a fairly early date, as we shall see, and Dorothea embraced the young artists' cause wholeheartedly. In a letter to Johannes of 1815 she assured her sons of her full support and expressed confidence in their success: "Something must surely come of your efforts to resacralize art, lead it back to God and the service of His Church, and recapture it from those who have misused it for irrelevant purposes and made an empty trifle out of what ought always to be sanctified. When did God ever abandon those who have dedicated themselves to His service?"[124] Inevitably, even before she met him, she took a keen interest

[119] "Es giebt keine Malerkunst, wenn man das Christentum nicht kennt. Wer nicht glaubt, hofft, und liebt, für den ist die Natur eine Wildniss, in welcher er nichts sieht als sich selber, für den ist also auch die Kunst nur ein eitler Spiegel seiner hochmüthigen Einbildung" (*Dorothea v. Schlegel geb. Mendelssohn und deren Söhne Johannes und Philipp Veit:Briefwechsel* [as in note 25], 1: 326, letter to Jonas Veit, dated Vienna, 11.2.1809).

[120] Ibid. 1: 420, letter dated Vienna, 30.5.1810.

[121] Ibid., 1: 307, letter dated Cologne, 2.11.1808.

[122] Ibid., 1: 428-29, letter dated Vienna, 15.8.1810.

[123] Ibid., 2: 55, letter from Friedrich Schlegel to Johannes Veit in Rome, dated Vienna, 23.10.1811.

[124] "Euer Bestreben, die Kunst wieder zu heiligen und sie wieder auf Gott und den Dienst seiner Kirche zurückzuführen und sie, die immer geheiligt bleiben sollte, den Händen derer wieder zu entreissen, die sie zu losen Dingen missbrauchten und ein leeres Unding aus ihr formte, kann ja nicht ohne Folgen bleiben; wann hätte Gott diejenigen verlassen, die sich seinem Dienst weihten?" (Ibid., 2: 316, letter of 18.8.1815).

in Overbeck's conversion to Catholicism, of which she tells Johannes she heard through the neoclassical Tyrolese artist Anton Koch, an early champion of the young painters in Rome. If it is true, she writes, "dann kann ich sagen, dass mich lange nichts so erfreut hat" ["I can say that nothing has pleased me so much in a long time"] and she asks Johannes to convey to Overbeck her and Friedrich's best wishes and warmest sympathy.[125] Later, during her stay in Rome, Overbeck was a frequent visitor to the Schlegels' house and it was there that he met his future wife, Nina Schiffengruber-Hartl, whom Dorothea regarded virtually as a daughter.[126] It was likewise at Dorothea's urging that Friedrich Schlegel responded in print to attacks on the Nazarenes, such as the notorious *Über die neue deutsche religiös-patriotische Kunst* by Goethe and his friend Johann Meyer (1817).

It was from another converted Jew, the newly appointed Prussian Consul-General to the Italian states, Jacob Salomon-Bartholdy, the son of a Berlin banker, that – as already noted – the young Nazarene artists received their first major commission in 1815 **(Pf. 34)**. As it happens, Bartholdy was related by marriage to Dorothea Schlegel, the latter's brother, Abraham Mendelssohn, having married Bartholdy's sister, Lea Salomon, in what Dorothea observed was a financially highly advantageous union for her brother. Lea and her husband had both been well educated and were fine musicians **(Pf. 35)**; their children achieved European renown, one as the composer Felix Mendelssohn, the other, his younger sister, Fanny, as a gifted pianist; and their palatial home in Berlin was frequented by some of the most distinguished men in Prussia at the time – among them the classicist August Böckh, the neoclassical sculptor Gottfried Schadow (the father of Overbeck's friend, the Nazarene painter Wilhelm Schadow), and the future historian of Hellenistic Greece and of modern Prussia, Gustav Droysen, whom the Mendelssohns had had the good sense to hire, when he was still an impoverished student, to be the tutor of their son Felix and who maintained a lifelong friendship with his pupil as well as the highest regard for the parents. A protégé and confidential adviser of the Prussian

[125]Ibid., 2: 229, letter to Johannes in Florence, dated Vienna, 11.12.1813.

[126]Nina had been unsuccessfully pursued by A.W. Schlegel and then in Rome by J.N. Ringseis, Ludwig of Bavaria's physician (Niebuhr, *Briefe: Neue Folge* [as in note 105], 1: 322, letter 125, to Savigny, 20.6.1818). Characteristically, the firmly Protestant Louise Seidler characterized Nina as a "fanatische Katholikin" who with her "sentimental, almost excessively melting beauty, . . . talent for intrigue . . . rich culture, familiarity with the Italian poets, and enthusiasm for art had somehow ensnared the "innocent" Overbeck (*Erinnerungen und Leben* [as in note 25], pp. 237-40). Overbeck's father tried to find out something about her from Niebuhr, who responded reassuringly (*Briefe: Neue Folge*, 1: 311, letter 123, to Overbeck, 13.6.1818) that she was universally praised for her intelligence and grace and clearly loved Overbeck, since she had preferred him, even though he had no money, to "a very wealthy and highly qualified man" (i.e., Ringseis). He described the betrothal more bluntly a few days later to Savigny as a "Hungerehe" (*Briefe: Neue Folge*, 1: 322, letter 125, 20.6.1818).

minister Hardenberg,[127] and, in the manner of almost all well-to-do Berlin Jews of the time, cultivated, talented, and patriotic, Bartholdy had distinguished himself, like Philipp Veit, in active service against the French and had been severely wounded at the battle of Ebersberg in 1809; he had written a history of the Tyrolean uprising against Napoleon's Bavarian allies – a highly popular cause in the Viennese family circle of his aunt, Fanny von Arnstein, at whose home he was a frequent visitor in those years – and dedicated it to the Czar[128]; he kept up a lively correspondence with his gifted young niece Fanny Mendelssohn, who later married Wilhelm Hensel, an artist close to the Nazarenes; he was a serious collector of antiquities (a manuscript essay, in French, on the colored glass of the Ancients was found among his papers after his death) and he had traveled to Greece and written one of the earliest modern accounts of the country.[129] He even contributed a short article on Sicilian folksongs, with texts, to the *Berliner Musicalische Zeitung* (no. 5, 1805), the first important musical journal in Berlin. He appears to have been eager to promote German art and support German artists.

In 1815, shortly after his arrival in Rome, he invited Overbeck, Cornelius, Wilhelm Schadow, and his nephew Philipp Veit, to decorate some rooms in his Roman residence in the Palazzo Zucchari **(Pf. 36)**. The theme of the frescoes produced for Bartholdy by the four young German painters was the Old Testament Joseph story. It has been said that this subject matter was chosen in deference to Bartholdy's Jewish origin. Most probably it was chosen because the Joseph story was usually interpreted – as in Pforr's *Entry of Rudolf of Habsburg into Basel in 1273* – as an anticipation of the story of Christ. As such, it underlined the continuity of the Old and New Testaments and marked a full acknowledgment of the founding role of the former, even while reaffirming the standard Christian position that the message of the Old Testament was given its full meaning only in the New Testament. The reconciliation of the Old and the New faiths implied by the Joseph frescoes was thus certainly

[127]It may have been Wilhelm von Humboldt (whom Bartholdy could easily have met at one of the Berlin Jewish salons frequented by both) who first recommended Bartholdy to Hardenberg. (Wilhelm von Humboldt, *Politische Briefe*, ed. W. Richter, vol. 1 [1935] p. 374, letter 348, from Humboldt to Hardenberg, Vienna, 4.4.1813): "Mr. Bartholdy me prie de dire un mot en sa faveur à Votre Excellence, et je puis le faire en bonne conscience. Il a des connaissances solides, du savoir-faire et de très-bons sentiments dans lesquels je ne l'ai jamais vu varier." In Hardenberg's own *Tagebücher* or diaries, "Bartoldi" appears quite frequently as participating in the negotiations with France for the withdrawal of allied troops, and as Hardenberg's guide in Rome during his visit there in 1821 (*Karl August von Hardenberg 1750-1822. Tagebücher und autobiographische Aufzeichnungen*, Thomas Stramm-Kuhlmann, ed. [Munich: Harald Boldt Verlag im R. Oldenbourg Verlag, 2000], pp. 960, 962, 964-65).

[128]*Der Krieg der Tyroler Landleute im Jahre 1809* (Berlin: Julius Hitzig, 1814). On the popularity of the Tyrolean uprising in the Arnstein circle, see Hilde Spiel, *Fanny von Arnstein: Daughter of the Enlightenment 1758-1818*, trans. Christine Shuttleworth (Oxford/New York: Berg, 1991; orig. German 1978), pp. 222-25.

[129]*Bruchstücke zur näheren Kenntnis des heutigen Griechenlandes* (Berlin, 1805). A French translation appeared in Paris in 2 volumes in 1807: *Voyage en Grèce fait dans les années 1801 et 1806 par J.L.S. Bartholdy* (Paris: Dentu, 1807).

achieved on terms favorable to Christianity, but it was a message of reconciliation nonetheless and thus, the four young artists might have thought, especially appropriate to Salomon-Bartholdy as a converted Jew. The interest of some Nazarene painters in Old Testament subjects has been noted by at least one art historian.[130] Could it be that this reflected a more general preoccupation with reconciliation and conversion?

Bartholdy has been accused of having driven a hard bargain and of paying the artists barely enough to live on, and not even enough to cover their expenses for materials.[131] However, the charge – its banal anti-Semitic character is hardly mistakable – comes chiefly from Niebuhr, who disliked "the Hardenberg Jew"[132] intensely and, as Prussian envoy to the Pope, resented the confidence "our illustrious Jew-lover" (as he termed Hardenberg[133]) apparently placed in a rival diplomat. Whatever the facts of the case, Bartholdy's initial gesture of support was crucial. It was the frescoes at the "Casa Bartholdy" (**Pf. 37-40**) that put the Nazarene painters on the map for the first time and won them an important commission from the Italian nobleman Count Carlo Massimi to decorate his Roman residence, as well as a commission from the Vatican itself, thanks to the intervention of a sympathetic Canova.[134]

Overbeck was especially close to the two Veit brothers, both of whom, as art students in Berlin and Dresden, had independently turned against the baroque and rococo tradition. The younger and subsequently more successful, Philipp (**Pf. 41**), who at one point took lessons from Caspar David Friedrich, complained to his mother of being forced by his teacher in Dresden, Matthäi, to copy Rubens. This, Dorothea Schlegel explained in a letter to her other son, was "a true mortification for Philipp, who does not like Rubens."[135] As for Jonas or Johannes (**Pf. 42**), he considered C.D. Friedrich "the only artist I know who follows the right road and does not try simply to provide pleasure by means of certain forms, but instead expresses the uniqueness of his own

[130]Wilhelm Schlink, "Heilsgeschichte in der Malerei der Nazarener" (see note 48).

[131]Niebuhr, *Briefe: Neue Folge* (as in note 105), 1: 210-11, letter 65, to his Berlin publisher G.A. Reimer, 14.8.1817. "Dieser Halunke gilt bey Hardenberg, und wohl überhaupt in Berlin, für einen edlen Beförderer der Künste!" ["This scoundrel passes with Hardenberg and in Berlin generally for a noble patron of the arts!"] exclaims the wrathful classical scholar and diplomat (p. 211).

[132]*Briefe: Neue Folge*, 1: 471, letter 215, to Frau Dora Hensler, 17.9.1819, p. 471.

[133]Bartholdy, according to Niebuhr, was "ein Männchen nach dem Herzen unsers durchlauchtigen Judenliebhabers." ["a little man after the heart of our eminent and distinguished Jew-lover"] (*Briefe: Neue Folge*, 1: 474, letter 216, to the Crown Prince of Prussia, 25.9.1819).

[134]On 2 July 1818 August Wilhelm Schlegel wrote from Heidelberg to Auguste de Stael, the son of Madame de Stael: "Nos artistes allemands commencent à avoir une grande vogue en Italie. Overbeck fait une série de tableaux tirés du Tasse pour un seigneur romain [Count Massimi] – Cornelius devait faire des scènes du Dante, mais il est rappelé pour exécuter de grands travaux en Allemagne, et le beaufils de mon frère [Philipp Veit] est chargé maintenant de peindre à Fresque une salle du Palais Massimi, en tirant ses sujets du Dante" (Körner, *Krisenjahre der Frühromantik* [as in note 99], 2:308-309).

[135]*Dorothea v. Schlegel geb. Mendelssohn und deren Söhne Johannes und Philipp Veit: Briefwechsel* (as in note 25), 2: 29, Dorothea to Johannes Veit in Rome, from Vienna, 21.5.1811.

being in pure, simple tones."[136] After some mentoring by Schinkel in Berlin, Johannes left for Rome in February 1811. His traveling companion on the Italian part of the journey was Josef Wintergerst, one of the founding members of the *Lukasbund*, who having been unable to make the journey to Rome with his fellow-rebels from the Vienna Academy in the previous year, was now on his way to join them. The young Veit's aim at the time was to take lessons with Gottlieb Schick, the neo-classical Württemberg painter who was much admired in the circle of the Schlegels and the Humboldts. On his way south, however, in Venice, he encountered and was overwhelmed by the fifteenth-century art of Giovanni Bellini **(Pf. 43, 44)**. He described the experience as a kind of conversion. "A few pictures by Johannes Bellinus that have escaped the greedy thievery [i.e., Napoleon's seizure of art works in the conquered territories] and destruction of our times and that still enjoy the benefit, in a few old churches, of remaining in their original home, have completely won my love," he wrote his mother, Dorothea, then still in Vienna. "In a few illuminating moments they showed me the path I have to travel and the goal I must strive toward. I would be fortunate indeed if I could firmly and joyfully seize upon what Heaven has revealed to me, as in a dream, through one of its saints. Were it not that I myself feel an urge within me to try and produce something similar, I would gladly end my life in prayer before such a painting." Indeed, if he does not find what he is looking for in Rome, he explains, he will return to Venice in order to study, in Bellini, "art in its simplest dress" ["die Kunst in ihrem schlichten Gewande"].[137] To his father Simon Veit, in Berlin, he explained that the deepest experiences of his journey to Rome had been provoked by seeing works by the early Italian painters: Bellinis in Venice, Giottos in Padua, and Francesco Francias in Bologna. Among painters whose works he had seen and been impressed by in the Roman galleries, he singled out for special mention Dürer and Lucas van Leyden. Johannes Veit's tastes thus ran in the same direction as those of the Nazarenes even before he knew

[136]Ibid., 2: 2, Johannes Veit in Vienna to Henriette Herz in Berlin, 1.1.1811. Johannes's high opinion of Friedrich was shared by his father, the banker Simon Veit. When he saw some of Friedrich's landscapes in Berlin, Veit wrote, "I stood in front of them for hours with feelings of rapture and awe.... Thanks, a thousand thanks to this unknown friend for the joyful and pleasant hours that he has vouchsafed to the rest of us through his noble spirit and handiwork" ["In entzückendem und heiligem Gefühle stand ich stundenlang davor... Dank, tausend Dank dem unbekannten Freund für die frohen und angenehmen Stunden, die er dem Menschen durch seinen Geist und seiner Hände Arbeit macht!"] (Ibid., 1:441-43, Simon Veit to his son Philipp in Dresden, Berlin, 2.12.1810) Henriette Herz expressed similar enthusiasm (Ibid., 1: 433-34).

[137]"Einige Bilder von Johannes Bellinus, welche der gierigen Raubsucht und der Zerstörung der Zeit entgangen, sich in einigen alten Kirchen noch ihres heimatlichen Daseins erfreuen, besitzen meine ganze Liebe. Sie haben mir in einigen lichtvollen Momenten den Weg, den ich zu gehen, und das Ziel gezeigt, und glücklich wäre ich, wenn ich mit frohem Muthe fest ergreifen könnte, was mir der Himmel durch einen seiner Heiligen wie im Traume offenbart hat... Wenn ich nicht selbst noch einen Trieb in mir fühlte, etwas ähnliches hervorbringen zu wollen, so könnte ich im Gebete vor so einem Bilde mein Leben enden" (*Dorothea v. Schlegel geb. Mendelssohn und deren Söhne Johannes und Philipp Veit:Briefwechsel* (as in note 25), 2: 14, Johannes Veit to Dorothea Schlegel in Vienna, from Venice, 12.3.1811). See also a letter from Johannes to his father, written from Venice on the same day, 12.3.1811 (ibid., 2: 16).

anything of them or their aspirations. Thanks no doubt to Wintergerst, he appears to have been introduced to the *Lukasbrüder* immediately on his arrival in the eternal city. If there had been room, he told his father, he would have been put up at the convent of San Isidoro where they were all staying.[138]

By the time Johannes Veit got to Rome, he no longer found Schick's neoclassical response to the baroque and rococo sufficient. Schick was seriously ill, he wrote to his mother in Vienna, and could not provide much guidance, but in any case the works by Schick that he had seen in Rome had disappointed him. They were, he said, enjoining Dorothea not to let his negative judgment be known, "sehr griechisch" ["very Greek"]. In contrast, his enthusiasm for the young *Lukasbrüder* – "my outstanding friends Vogel and Overbeck" – was unbounded.[139] "I have been lucky enough to find an association of young artists here who stand out from all the others not only on account of their moral purity, but on account of the nature and quality of their work," he reported to his father in Berlin. "I have come as close to them as possible and consider myself fortunate to be able to work alongside them."[140] A letter to his mother in Vienna conveys the same enthusiasm. "What would you and Friedrich [i.e., Schlegel] only have to say about these young people, how delighted you would be to see before your eyes the venerable past ["die alte Zeit"] reborn in their pictures! I would never have imagined, after all the glorious works that I saw on my way here, that anything like this was awaiting me – and it is the work of young men as simple and tender-hearted as children."[141] Soon he has joined the group in their evening painting and discussion sessions at San Isidoro.[142] In Overbeck especially, he wrote to his father, he has found both a model to emulate and a friend. "I consider myself blessed in having found here a friend whose heavenly soul is a mirror of virtue and perfection, a human being whose like few are even capable of conceiving. He seems almost to have no contact with earthly things, and yet every one admires him and finds happiness in being close to him and longs for his love. The joyful serenity of a higher life breathes in his paintings and yet everything is comprehended so naturally and with such truth. . . . He is a year younger than I am and yet I consider him already at this point the most important painter since the time of Raphael."[143] Two months later he explains that he has been fully adopted by the group of young German artists he has written about, that they can all hardly contain their joy when they get together, and that he is experiencing to the full the happiness of friendship. He hopes that he might even be inducted into the *Bund*

[138]Ibid., 2:25, Letter dated Rome, 30.4.1818.
[139]Ibid., 2: 21, Johannes Veit to Dorothea Schlegel in Vienna, from Rome, 24.4.1811.
[140]Ibid., 2: 49. Johannes Veit to Simon Veit in Berlin, Rome, 4.9.1811.
[141]Ibid., 2: 21, Johannes Veit to Dorothea Schlegel in Vienna, from Rome, 24.4.1811.
[142]Ibid., 2: 57-58. Johannes Veit to Simon Veit in Berlin, Rome, 29.12.1811.
[143]Ibid., 2: 93, Johannes Veit to Simon Vet in Berlin, Rome, 7.7.1812.

in place of "a faithful brother" (i.e., Pforr) who has succumbed to tuberculosis. Once again he speaks of Overbeck with enthusiasm: "I cannot tell you how much more attached to him I become with every passing day. In this remarkable young man I have found my model in every single respect." He now has the pleasant prospect, he adds, of being able to live with him on a permanent basis, since his landlord has several additional rooms for rent in his house.[144]

Toward the end of the year (1812) Johannes explained to his father in greater detail that what drew him to Overbeck, besides the latter's infinite sweetness of character, was the fact that he was already on the way toward realizing goals that he, Johannes, had begun to articulate but had so far been incapable of acting on.

> Even though any insightful person has to admit that, since Raphael, art has been in continuous decline down to our own times, this is acknowledged by artists only in very general terms, whereas among painters especially, no one in particular has yet resolved to abandon the old routines or once dared to attempt something better. The reason for this is not hard to find: it is always very difficult to leave a well-trodden path and to strike out on a new one that one has to define for oneself. I had already become aware of this in Dresden. I was astonished to see in the works of Holbein, Leonardo, Dürer, and Bellini how the same striving united all those artists, like their age itself, despite the fact that they lived very far from each other and scarcely knew each other's names. Since that time, my only wish has been to get close to those great luminaries. But I found it almost impossible to tear myself away from an artistic practice that I unfortunately learned from the beginning, and all my efforts would assuredly have remained fruitless had a good spirit not brought me to Italy. . . . Almost every church here that survives from the glorious and misunderstood Middle Ages is an eloquent reminder of the grandeur and power that through their union in the holy Mass remain active in us down to the present time and that will turn the spark of a better art into a flaming torch, provided we persist in pursuing that goal. How astonished I was when I found that these thoughts, which had been awakened in me most forcefully in the course of my journey, had already been acted upon here in Rome by someone else, by a young man who, though superior to us all in wit and talent, is on the outside the most modest of us all and who in the simplest form conceals the most affectionate soul. You can imagine how powerfully I am drawn to him. My sole ambition is to raise my still cold and uncouth nature up to the level of his. His approval has become my greatest reward.[145]

[144]Ibid., 2: 101, Johannes Veit to Simon Veit in Berlin, Rome, September 1812.
[145]Ibid., 2: 115, Johannes Veit to Simon Veit in Berlin, from Rome, November 1812.

In the same letter we learn that he is now living with Overbeck, Colombo (the only Italian to be inducted into the *Lukasbund*), and Wintergerst; that he is "every day more attached" to them; and that they are his "models in art." The veneration Overbeck inspired in Johannes was sufficiently unusual for Philipp Veit, then still in Vienna, to be puzzled by his brother's extreme regard for a young artist, who was himself still far from being fully accomplished.[146] Later, however, when Philipp too had become a close friend and admirer of Overbeck's, he painted a double portrait of Overbeck and Johannes **(Fig. XV, Pf. 45)**. Johannes's devotion to Overbeck was expressed in practical as well as verbal and artistic terms. He did indeed treat his friends "wie meine Brüder und Vorgesetzte" ["as my brothers and superiors"].[147] When Metternich's Viennese banker and friend, Leopold Herz, commissioned him to buy something for him in Rome, Johannes tried to interest Herz in a *Madonna with Sleeping Child* by Overbeck **(Pf. 46)**, which, he told his father, had attracted much attention in Rome and for which the artist was asking 12 ducats.[148] After it

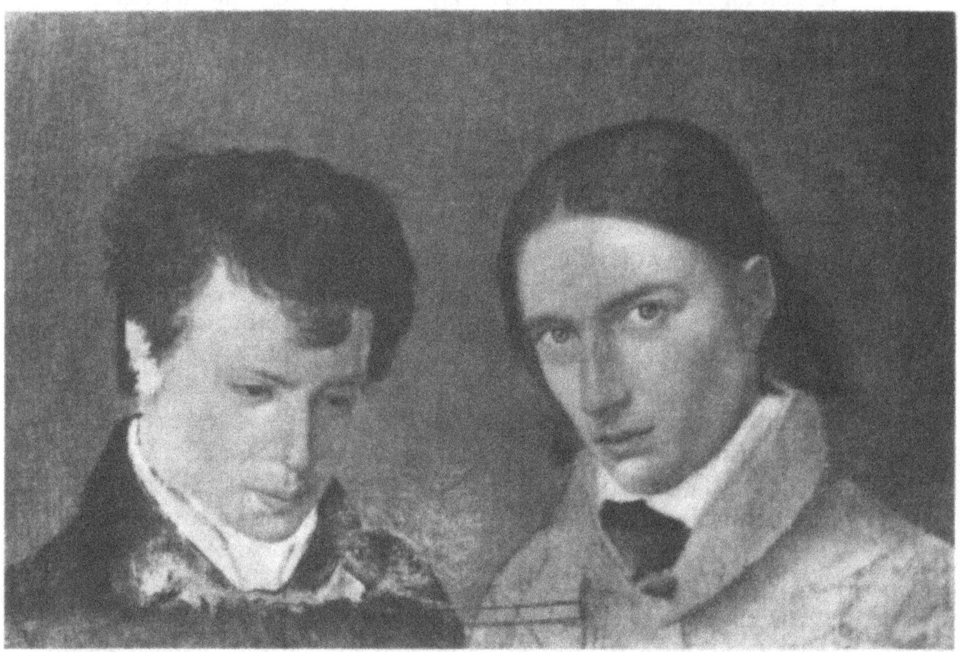

Fig. XV. Philipp Veit. *Doppelporträt Johannes Veit und Friedrich Overbeck.* (1816). Oil on canvas. 34 × 51.5 cm. Unsigned. Originally in Städtische Gemäldegalerie, Mainz (inv. No. 783); destroyed in a fire at the Munich Glaspalast in 1931. From a reproduction in Martin Spahn, *Philipp Veiti* (Bielefeld and Leipzig: Velhagen & Klasing, 1901), fig. 19, p. 23.

[146]Ibid., 2: 119, Philipp Veit to Simon Veit in Berlin, Vienna, 30.12.1812.
[147]Ibid., 2: 130. Johannes veit to Simon Veit in Berlin, Rome, 1,1,1813.
[148]Ibid., 2: 57-58. Johannes veit to Simon Veit in Berlin, Rome, 29.12.1811.

became clear that Herz was not interested in purchasing the work, Johannes appealed to his father to step into the breach,[149] and it seems that Veit was willing to oblige. He appears to have paid 20 ducats for the painting.[150] When Wintergerst ran out of funds at one point, Johannes again intervened to help out. He commissioned his friend to make copies of ceiling paintings in the Vatican and undertook to pay him for them out of his own funds, in the hope that buyers might ultimately be found for well-executed copies and that he would thus be able in due course to recoup the money he had laid out. (In the event, the physical difficulty of working on scaffolding in the dark and damp of winter brought on a fever and there was fear for a time that Wintergerst would go the way of Pforr.) From a letter to his father of September 4, 1811, it appears that when Overbeck's father, the Lübeck senator, "lost his position as a result of the recent changes" (i.e., the incorporation of Lübeck into the French Empire) and was thus no longer able to provide his son with the modest subsidies he needed to support his career as an artist, Johannes immediately sounded Veit out about doing something for "his best friend" in order that he should not have to resort to seeking out "Brodarbeiten" ("commissions that will bring in money"). "What a loss it would be for art," he wrote, "if this talented and – in his daily life – saintly individual were to be blocked from pursuing his proper career."[151] A letter of 23 October 1814, suggests that Johannes may have persuaded Veit, who was well known for his generosity – Dorothea even paid poetic tribute to him for it, doubtless hoping thereby to ensure its continuation[152] – to give Overbeck some direct financial support: "Your willingness to support Overbeck with a pension has pleased me as well as other friends, to whom he has spoken of it, immensely. For us it is yet another demonstration of the goodness of your heart." Johannes hastens to assure his father that his generosity has been well placed and that Overbeck is a worthy object of his "Mildthätigkeit." Though Overbeck has helped him in many ways, he explains, "he has repeatedly refused to accept any monetary

---

[149]Ibid., 2: 105, Dorothea Schlegel to Johannes Veit in Rome, Vienna, 16.10.1812; 2: 115, Johannes Veit to Simon Veit in Berlin, Rome, November 1812.

[150]Howitt, 2: 401.

[151]*Dorothea v. Schlegel geb. Mendelssohn und deren Söhne Johannes und Philipp Veit:Briefwechsel* (as in note 25), 2: 49, letter from Johannes Veit to Simon Veit in Berlin, from Rome, 4.9.1811.

[152]In Dorothea's Tagebuch for 1810, there is a poem addressed to her former husband praising him for having always acted uprightly in his business affairs, never exploited anybody, and consistently demonstrated his generosity. The last line reads: "He stores his wealth only to disburse it more abundantly" (*Dorothea v. Schlegel geb. Mendelssohn und deren Söhne Johannes und Philipp Veit:Briefwechsel*, 1:448) In a letter to his son Philipp in Dresden, Veit himself spelled out his philosophy of generosity. He has never considered his sons spendthrifts, he writes, just because they ask for money and has never begrudged them any sum that was for a good purpose. Indeed, he hopes that they will learn from his example "the art of giving money away at the right moment." "I myself was never a spendthrift," he adds; "nor, however, was I tightfisted, and I can truly say that I got far more pleasure in the course of my life from giving money away than from making it" (ibid, 1:401-444, to Philipp Veit in Dresden, from Berlin, 13.1.1810). Educated Jews like Simon Veit, his former wife, and his sons, clearly had to struggle against a different popular image of the Jew – the one manifested in Niebuhr's criticism of the way Bartholdy treated the artists who worked for him.

assistance from me. Still, as I know he has some pressing debts, I have given him 25 scudi to help out with the worst. I had great difficulty getting him to accept this money, however, and in any case he will accept it only as a loan, to be repaid as soon as he receives payment from the Queen of Bavaria, for whom he has produced a painting." This almost "excessive scrupulousness," Johannes explained, is what keeps Overbeck in worse shape financially than many far less talented artists.[153] Overbeck himself expressed his gratitude to Johannes for many kindnesses. "I am already so deeply in your debt," he wrote to him on one occasion, "and you keep piling ever more acts of generosity on top of those you have already performed. What should I say, how should I thank you for so many gifts, as well as for what motivates your generosity, your love and friendship for me?"[154]

Not the least of the bonds that united the son of the Senator from Lübeck and the son of the Berlin Jewish merchant-banker was their common experience of conversion.[155] In one letter, after first expressing relief that young Veit has recovered from a physical illness, Overbeck passes to an even more important improvement in his friend's psychological and spiritual condition (Johannes's moodiness had long been a source of alternating irritation and anxiety for his mother and stepfather), which he describes, in what was probably an allusion to Jonas's conversion, as a "rebirth." He then proceeds to tell of his own conversion.

> You have recovered physically – that is already a lot. Thank God for it! But then – you have also been reborn in your inmost humanity, you have found new joy in nature, God's creation, and a new trust in other human beings that allows you to associate lovingly with them – and you now walk without weariness but rather with a gentle and quiet spirit before the Lord! . . . I would add about myself that by the grace of God I have now been truly taken back into the bosom of the Church. Palm Sunday was the – for me – unforgettable day on which I was admitted into the Holiness of the Lord . . . It happened very quietly in a little chapel in the Collegio Romano but my heart was full to bursting.

[153]Ibid., 2: 285-86, Johannes Veit to Simon Veit in Berlin, from Rome, 23.10.1814.

[154]Ibid, 2: 198-99, Friedrich Overbeck to Johannes Veit in Florence, from Rome, 27.8.1813.

[155]In addition, Johannes Veit's godfather at his baptism had been Stolberg, whom Overbeck revered (Hempel [as in note 32], pp. 237-38, notes 705, 706).

The letter ends with an appeal and a blessing: "Pray for me, dear friend. And for my parents and siblings, pray that He may shed the light of His grace on them too. May God's grace be with you!"[156]

The common experience of conversion – Veit's from Judaism **(Pf. 47)**, his own from Protestantism – was perceived by Overbeck as both a bond between them personally and a promise of that future union of all humankind in a single Church, which the Pietists of the previous century never allowed to slip from their view. One cannot help wondering whether Overbeck might not have displaced on to his Catholicism a good deal of the ardent longing for Parousia that Lutheran orthodoxy seems to have successfully wrung out of Pietism over the years. In the already quoted letter of 27 August 1813, thanking Johannes for many kindnesses, Overbeck evokes a condition of unity and brotherhood strongly reminiscent of that which seventeenth and early-eighteenth-century Pietists expected to follow the final conversion of the Jews and the reunification of all the different faiths and churches in the one true Church – and curiously similar to that which had inspired the Utopian plan for a colony in Tahiti that his own father had dreamed up in earlier years.

> Ah, dear friend, what might we humans not be for each other, how might we not help and encourage each other toward good ends, how not bind the Lord close to us through mutual love, harmony, tolerance, so that the earth might be a forecourt of Heaven. And of how little help we are to each other, for the most part, how often we even stand in each other's way! But we, who have been called by the same mercy to the same glory, out of the darkness of a life devoid of spirit and given over to all kinds of desires into the light of faith, let us grow and increase until we arrive at a single faith and knowledge and make of ourselves a spiritual dwelling place where God will dwell with us in spirit.[157]

---

[156] "Du bist körperlich genesen – das ist schon ein Grosses! Gott sei Dank! – Dann aber – Du bist am inneren Menschen wiedergeboren, hast neue Freudigkeit gewonnen an der herrlichen Natur, der Schöpfung Gottes! hast neues Vertrauen zu den Menschen erlangt, Dich liebevoll zu ihnen zu gesellen und – wandelst unermüdet in sanftem und stillem Geist vor dem Herrn! . . . Von mir setze ich noch hinzu, dass mich der Gnade Gottes nunmehr wirklich in den Schoss der Kirche zurückgeführt hat. Der Palmensonntag war der unvergessliche Tag für mich, wo ich eintrat in den Heiligthum des Herrn . . . Ganz im Stillen geschah es in einer kleinen Kapelle im Collegio Romano, aber in meinem Herzen war grosses Gespränge!" "Bete für mich, mein Lieber! Und für meine Eltern und Geschwister, dass Er sie mit dem Lichte der Gnade erleuchten wollte. – Die Gnade Gottes mit Dir!" (*Dorothea v. Schlegel geb. Mendelssohn und deren Söhne Johannes und Philipp Veit:Briefwechsel* (as in note 25), 2: 167, Friedrich Overbeck to Johannes Veit in Orvieto, from Rome, 5.5.1813).

[157] "Ach! Mein Lieber, was könnten wir Menschen einander nicht alles sein, wie könnten wir einander helfen und fördern zu allen Guten, wie könnten wir durch gegenseitige Liebe, Eintracht, Duldung, den Herrn unter uns fesseln, dass die Erde ein Vorhof des Himmels wäre; und wie wenig sind wir einander meistens, ja wie hinderlich sind wir einander oft! Wir aber, die wir durch gleiche Barmherzigkeit berufen sind zu gleicher Herrlichkeit, aus der Finsterniss des ungeistlichen Lebens in allerlei Lüsten zu dem Lichte des Glaubens, . . . lass uns wachsen und zunehmen, bis dass wir herankommen zu einerlei Glauben und Erkenntnis und uns bauen zu einem geistlichen Hause, zur Behausung Gottes im Geiste." (*Dorothea v. Schlegel geb. Mendelssohn und deren Söhne Johannes und Philipp Veit:Briefwechsel* (as in note 25), 2: 198-99, Friedrich Overbeck to Johannes veit in Florence, from Rome, 27.8.1813).

If Overbeck's interest in the Old Testament figure of Sulamith as early as 1809/1810 had been based chiefly on his view of his vocation as an artist, he now, three years later, had other grounds for identifying with the bride of the Song of Songs – in his own conversion and in the conversion experience that he shared with Jewish friends like the Veit brothers and their mother.

As to the thoughts or feelings he might have had concerning Jews in general, there is not much documentary evidence. As is well known, there was a sharp rise in xenophobic nationalism and anti-Semitism in the German lands in the years immediately following the War of Liberation, not least in Overbeck's native Lübeck. This occurred despite the fact that Austrian and German Jews had been actively engaged in the war[158] **(Pf. 48)**. However, there is no sign anywhere in Overbeck's work either of the popular anti-Jewish sentiments that inspired mobs of peasants and artisans to burn down Jewish homes in the notorious "Hep-Hep" riots – denounced by the poet Voss, the intimate friend of Overbeck Senior, as a regression to the worst times of the Middle Ages[159] – or of the less vulgar and brutal anti-Semitism expressed in Overbeck's own milieu by friends such as Clemens Brentano, one of the founding members of

[158]Many young Jews had volunteered – 15,000, according to one source, in Austria alone; fifty-five Prussian Jewish officers are said to have fallen at Waterloo; between 1813 and 1815 seventy-two were awarded the Iron Cross; Salomon-Bartholdy and Philipp Veit both won official recognition for their bravery in action; while in Vienna, Fanny von Arnstein, the daugher of the wealthy Berlin banker Daniel Itzig, played a leading role in organizing support for wounded and disabled soldiers, as well as for the leaders of the Tyrolese peasant revolt. Quoting Franz Joseph Jekel, *Pohlens Staatsveränderungen und letzte Verfassung*, 6 vols. (1803-1810), 2: 58, Friedrich Schlegel claims that "die Juden haben sich in dem ungeendigten Kriege – darin freywillige Kriegsbeyträge besonders ausgezeichnet, über 15,000 Israeliten dienten theils als Soldaten, theils als Fuhrwesensknechte unter Oesterreichischen Fahnen" ["the Jews specially distinguished themselves in the unfinished war by their voluntary contributions; under the Austrian flag alone, over 15,000 Jews served partly as soldiers, partly as humble carters"] ("Zur Geschichte und Politik" [1815], *Kritische Friedrich Schlegel Ausgabe,* Ernst Behler, ed. [as in note 100], 21:146). On Prussian Jews, see Meyer, *The Origins of the Modern Jew* (as in note 84), p. 139. On Fanny von Arnstein's activity in support of the war against Napoleon, see Hilde Spiel, *Fanny von Arnstein: Daughter of the Enlightenment, 1758-1818* (as in note 128), pp. 224, 276-77). See also two works by Johann Ludwig Ewald, a Protestant pastor in Baden, who wrote in defence of Jewish emancipation in the Restoration period, evoking the patriotism and courage of the Jews in the national struggle against Napoleon: *Der Geist des Christenthums und des ächten deutschen Volksthums, dargestellt gegen die Feinde der Israeliten* (Carlsruhe: D.R. Marx'sche Buchhandlung, 1817) p. 88, and *Einige Fragen und auch nochmehr unlügbare Wahrheiten, Juden- und Menschenbildung betreffend* (Carlsruhe: D.R. Marx'sche Buchhandlung, 1820), p. 20. Both works are reproduced in Johann Ludwig Ewald, *Projüdische Schriften aus den Jahren 1817 bis 1821,* J.A. Steiger, ed. (Heidelberg: Mauritius Verlag, 2000).

[159]Voss observed that "one might have thought one was living in 1419, not 1819" quoted in Amos Elon, *The Pity of it All: A History of Jews in Germany 1743-1933* (New York: Metropolitan Books/Henry Holt, 2002), p. 102.

the celebrated Berlin *Tischgesellschaft*, the charter of which explicitly excluded Jews and women.[160]

Certainly there was no hostility to Jews in the household of Friedrich and Dorothea Schlegel – with both of whom, as have seen, Overbeck was closely associated in his early years in Rome. Fervent Catholic as he had become, Friedrich Schlegel almost always refers to Jews with respect and he played an active role in the difficult political and diplomatic negotiations that took place at the Congress of Vienna with a view to preserving and extending to all the German states the civil rights guaranteed to Jews by the Prussian edict of

[160]This issue is notoriously complex. Clemens Brentano and Fichte were both unfavorably disposed to Jews, to say the least, but not apparently to converted Jews. Both were close friends of Dorothea Schlegel, and Brentano was later something like an honorary member of the Veit household in Frankfurt. Brentano even identified, in some measure, with the figure of the homeless, wandering Jew. "Ich aber bin eine Gattung ewiger Jude der nicht lebt noch stirbt, und nun ewig wandelt, ohne zu handeln, zu schaffen, zu geniessen" (letter to Savigny, 1802, quoted in Hartwig Schultz, *Schwarzer Schmetterling: Zwanzig Kapitel aus dem Leben des romantischen Dichters Clemens* Brentano [Berlin: Berlin Verlag, 2000], p. 260). Despite some anti-Semitic comments that later made her a popular figure with the Nazis, Caroline von Humboldt fell in love in her mature years with the cultivated and widely traveled Jewish doctor David Koreff (see Gustav Sichelschmidt, *Caroline von Humboldt: Ein Frauenbild aus der Goethezeit* [Düsseldorf: Droste-Verlag, 1989], p. 146ff). Wilhelm von Humboldt himself, the pupil of Dohm and one of the most reliable and indefatigable champions of Jewish rights, expressed negative personal feelings about Jews (see Paul R. Sweet, *Wilhelm von Humboldt. A Biography* [Columbus: Ohio State University Press, 1980], 2 vols., 2:206-208). Even the case of Achim von Arnim, the author of some grossly threatening anti-Semitic satires, is somewhat more complex than a cursory reading of these writings would lead one to believe (see Heinz Härtl, "Romantischer Antisemitismus: Arnim und die 'Tischgesellschaft,' *Weimarer Beiträge*, 1987, 33: 1159-1173; also Hartwig Schultz, *Schwarzer Schmetterling*, pp. 255-61). On the other side, there is the ambivalence of many educated Jews, converted or not, toward their poorer and more observant fellow-Jews and toward Judaism itself, an ambivalence for which the anti-Semitism of the general society they wanted to belong to bears, of course, some responsibility. Dorothea Schlegel, for instance, resents the implication – in an article in the French *Moniteur*, on the eve of Napoleon's opening of the Sanhedrin or assembly of Jewish notables – that all Jews, except for enlightened Jews like her father Moses Mendelssohn, are usurers (*Dorothea v. Schlegel geb. Mendelssohn und deren Söhne Johannes und Philipp Veit: Briefwechsel* [as in note 25], 1: 168-69, Dorothea to Friedrich Schlegel, from Cologne, 3.7.1806); she expresses a mixture of impatience, compassion, and contempt when she tells August Wilhelm Schlegel, about a young man who goes by the name of Herr von Delmar and who hopes Schlegel will introduce him to Mme de Stael, that though the young man is perfectly upstanding and decent, he seems to fear nothing more than that people might discover that he was not always Herr von Delmar and is in fact a baptised nephew of the widow Levy, née Itzig – "as though his Christianity was spread too thin and the old Judaism underneath could be seen through it" (ibid., 2:82-83, Dorothea Schlegel to A.W. Schlegel at Coppet, from Vienna, 16.5.1812). But at the same time, she herself is amused and delighted not to have been recognized as Jewish and to have passed for a Spanish woman in the eyes of her fellow-travelers on a journey to Prague (ibid., 1: 305-307, Dorothea to her sons, from Prague, end of October, 1808); more significantly, she confesses her "horror" of Orthodox Judaism. As for her son Philipp, several distinctly, though perhaps not viciously anti-Semitic caricatures are attributed to him (see Peter Dittmar, *Die Darstellung der Juden in der populären Kunst zur Zeit der Emanzipation* [Munich/London/New York/Paris: K.G. Saur, 1992], pp. 137 [fig. 60] and 364 [fig. 214]). The classic study of Jewish ambivalence about Judaism and entrapment in the alternative between the conditions of pariah and parvenu is Hannah Arendt's *Rahel Varnhagen, The Life of a Jewess*, Richard and Clara Winston, trans., Liliane Weissberg, ed. (Baltimore: Johns Hopkins University Press, 1997; orig. German 1959).

1812.[161] Indeed, despite its obviously malicious intent, a Nazi literary historian's attribution of Schlegel's romantic esthetics to his growing association with Jews, the influence of the Berlin Jewish salons he frequented, and the "Jewish spirit" of Dorothea may well contain at least a grain of truth. There may be some inner connection (though not the simple cause-and-effect connection argued for by the scholar in question) between Schlegel's conversion to Catholicism, largely under the influence of his formerly Jewish wife, and his evolving ideas on the subject of religion, on the one hand, and his abandonment of previously held neoclassical esthetic principles and embrace of romantic ideals, on the other. Early in his career, Schlegel had indeed seemed to espouse a view of the world in which the strict maintenance of distinctions was the foundation of all good order. Thus, for instance, he had denounced the confusion of lyric and dramatic, the tendency to treat history as fiction and fiction as history, and, in general, the erasing of the boundaries on which the integrity of the various arts and genres was widely held to depend as a disastrous innovation of modernity. The start of his relationship with Dorothea coincided, in contrast, with his adopting and advocating a completely different view. Transgressing boundaries and bringing together what had previously been kept strictly separate was now seen as the primary task for modern man. The neoclassical world of the ancien regime was shocked by the smudging of the distinction between male and female in the novel *Lucinde* (1799), in which the male character recognizes his own femininity and the female has likewise some characteristics usually associated with the male. Soon Schlegel was promoting a new vision of poetry as "progressive Universalpoesie," the goal of which was "not only to reunite all the discrete genres of literary art and combine poetry with philosophy and rhetoric," but "to mix and at times fuse poetry and prose, creative genius and

[161]Schlegel appears to have been among those who saw a relationship between Germans and Jews as two peoples charged with a providential mission in history; see *Kritische Friedrich Schlegel Ausgabe* (as in note 100), 20: 312 (dated 1811 or 1812) and 22: 215 (dated 1824). Above all, he played a significant role in the campaign to have the Prussian emancipation edicts of 1812 accepted in principle by all the states in the German *Bund*; see *Kritische Ausgabe*, vol. 21:351-52 (Schlegel challenges Lübeck's resistance to application of the emancipation edicts) and 380-81 (Schlegel argues in a report to the Frankfurt Bundestag, 1816-1818, against the city of Frankfurt's refusal to apply the edicts). On the issue of Jewish emancipation at the Congress of Vienna, see Max J. Kohler, "Jewish Rights at the Congresses of Vienna (1814-1815) and Aix-la-Chapelle (1818)," *Publications of the American Jewish Historical Society*, 1918, 26: 33-125; on the provisions regarding Jewish rights in the draft German constitution drawn up for consideration by the Congress of Vienna in March 1815 by Friedrich Schlegel, at the time official Austrian service, see pp. 50-51; a useful, brief summary in Spiel, *Fanny von Arnstein* (as in note 128), pp. 292-97.

criticism, art poetry and popular poetry."[162] From Schlegel's new "catholic" perspective, all exclusions, boundaries and divisions that radically separate male and female, poetry and philosophy, imagination and reason – and why not also Jew and Christian? – could and would be overcome if each were willing to acknowledge that the other is not a stranger or an enemy but an integral part of itself. "Perhaps a complete new age of art and science would begin," he wrote in the closing years of the eighteenth century, "if nothing were separate and cut off any more, if more mutually complementary natures could come together and create in common. It is often impossible to resist the idea that two separate spirits might truly belong to each other, like sundered halves of a former unity, and that they can only fully realize themselves when united with each other."[163]

I have not been able to ascertain what position, if any, Overbeck took in the matter of Jewish civil rights, but it would have been difficult for him to be indifferent to it. Not only was Schlegel deeply involved in it, the Hansa cities (Hamburg, Bremen, and Overbeck's native Lübeck), along with Frankfurt-am-Main, were the most resistant to adopting the emancipation edict. The Lübeck Jews in particular, having been allowed to establish residence in the city only after it was incorporated into the French Empire as part of the department of Bouches de l'Elbe (until then, despite frequent pleas for residency rights, Jews had been confined to the nearby village of Moisling in the Danish-controlled Duchy of Holstein), were expelled from the city in 1818. What is certain is that Overbeck's father, who was Bürgermeister at the time of the expulsion, was an admirer of Moses Mendelssohn, had entertained friendly relations, while on his diplomatic missions to Paris, with the banker Berr Lion

[162]"In his 1795 essay he emphasizes the unchanging character of the eternal boundaries of poetry in opposition to modern literature, 'in which philosophy gets lost in the poetically vague and poetry inclines toward a bottomless brooding, in which history is treated like literature and literature like history, in which even the poetic genres change their definition, so that a lyrical mood becomes the subject of a drama and dramatic material is forced into the mold of lyrical expressiveness.' ['wo sich die Philosophie in das dichterisch Unbestimmte verliert und die Poesie sich zu einer grüblerischen Tiefe neigt, wo die Geschichte als Dichtung, diese aber als Geschichte behandelt wird, wo selbst die Dichtarten gegenseitig die Bestimmung wechseln, eine lyrische Stimmung Gegenstand eines Dramas wird, ein dramatischer Stoff in lyrische Form gezwängt wird.'] He faults modern poetry for lacking character and individuality and sees confusion and lawlessness as the hallmark of modern literature in general. In his essay 'Über die Grenzen des Schönen' ['On the limits of the beautiful'] we read: 'Our confusion is most obvious in art itself. One art spreads over into the domain of another and one genre into the domain of another.' ['Und eben in der Kunst ist auch unsere Verworrenheit am offenbarsten. Eine Kunst schweift in das Gebiet der anderen und eine Gattung in das Gebiet der anderen hinüber.'] Those words date from the year 1795. Let us compare with them the famous definition of romantic poetry in the *Athenaeum*: 'Romantic poetry is a progressively developing universal poetry. Its mission is not only to reunite all the separated genres of poetry and to bring poetry into contact with philosophy and rhetoric; it should and will also now mix, now fuse poetry and prose, original genius and criticism, art poetry and folk poetry' ['Die romantische Poesie ist eine progressive Universalpoesie. Ihre Bestimmung ist nicht bloss, alle getrennten Gattungen der Poesie wieder zu vereinigen und die Poesie mit der Philosophie und Rhetorik in Berührung zu setzen. Sie will und soll auch Poesie und Prosa, Genialität und Kritik, Kunstpoesie und Naturpoesie bald mischen, bald verschmelzen']" (Josef Veldtrup, "Friedrich Schlegel und die jüdische Geistigkeit," *Zeitschrift für Deutschkunde* [1938], 52: 401-414, at 406).

[163]*Athenaeum*, 1788-1800, Part 1, "Fragmente," quoted by Brigitte Heise, *Johann Friedrich Overbeck* (as in note 33), p. 76.

Fuld (or Fould) – with whom Humboldt also had connections – and in his private correspondence always wrote of his associations with Jews in a respectful tone.[164] Among the citizens of Lübeck (a restricted and privileged group of the total population, comprised of wealthy merchants and privileged artisans), most of the well-to-do and educated patricians, such as Overbeck's father, did what they could to resist the pressure from the artisans for drastic action against the Jews and then, in face of the artisans' insistence, tried – unsuccessfully – to get them to moderate the demand for total expulsion.[165] In addition, the eloquent Christian lawyer who undertook to present the case in favor of the Jews of the three Hanseatic cities at the Congress of Vienna, Carl August Buchholz, was a Lübecker from the family of the Syndicus of the Cathedral Chapter, Georg Friedrich Buchholz, a Dr. Juris and a music-lover like Christian Adolf himself, and one of the latter's closest friends as a young man. Admittedly, C.A. Buchholz's position – "Christians and Jews will clasp hands in untroubled brotherly love and join together in pursuit of the same goal, that of being good citizens of the state, which will embrace them all impartially with equal love"[166] – is essentially the same state-centered Enlightenment position that had been expressed more than a quarter of a century earlier in the classic tract, *über die bürgerliche Verbesserung der Juden* (1781; enlarged edition, 1783), by Christian Wilhelm Dohm, the mentor of the Humboldt brothers and one of the inspirers of state-chancellor Hardenberg's plans for Jewish emancipation. It was one with which, with his antimodernist bent, Overbeck might well not have sympathized. But Jewish emancipation was also supported by a fair number of sincere Christians whose faith had remained untinged by rationalism. Klopstock himself

[164]On Christian Adolf Overbeck's judgment of Moses Mendelssohn, see Heinz Jansen, *Aus dem Göttinger Hainbund* (as in note 12), p. 106; on Overbeck senior's frequenting of the Foulds in Paris, see *Beieinandersein ist das täglich Brot der Liebe. Briefe C.A. Overbecks*, Fritz Luchmann, ed. (as in note 11), p. 128, letter from Paris of 23.9.1807 ("Yesterday I had dinner at the house of the interesting Jewish family of Fould, where I also met Mendelssohn's sister, an excellent young woman" [more likely Mendelssohn's daughter, Jette or Henriette, who was living on the rue Richer at the time and running a school; Mendelssohn's son Abraham had served an apprenticeship with the Foulds in 1803]; on Wilhelm von Humboldt and Fould, see Frédéric Barbier, "Les Origines de la maison Fould: Berr Léon et Bénédict Fould (vers 1740-1804)," *Revue historique*, 1989, 281: 159-92, at p. 168.

[165]See the detailed accounts in Rabbi Dr. S. Carlebach, *Geschichte der Juden in Lübeck und Moisling* (n.p.n.d.), a series of nine lectures given in 1890-1898 with a foreword dated "Lübeck, December, 1898," and David Alexander Winter, *Geschichte der jüdischen Gemeinde in Moisling-Lübeck* (Lübeck: Max Schmidt-Römhild, 1968 [Veröffentlichungen zur Geschichte der Hansestadt Lübeck, 20]). The situation at the time of the decree of 14 February, 1818, expelling the Jews of Lübeck from the city, had been anticipated 120 years earlier, in 1699, when the *Bürgerschaft* (i.e., mostly artisans and tradespeople) demanded – and obtained – the expulsion of the Jews, against the general inclination of the majority of the merchants in the *Rat* or Senate.

[166]"In ungetrübter Liebe werden Christen und Israeliten sich die Bruderhände darbieten, und zu dem schönen Zwecke sich vereinen, *gute Bürger* des Staates zu seyn, welcher sie alle mit gleicher unpartheyischer Liebe umfassen wird." (Quoted by Franklin Kopitzsch, "Grundprinzipe und Probleme der lübeckschen Geschichte im 18/19 Jahrhundert: Lübecks Weg in die moderne Zeit," in *Neue Forschungen zur Geschichte der Hansestadt*, A. Grassmann Lübeck, ed. [Lübeck: Max Schmidt-Römhild, 1985], pp. 63-75, on p. 72. The title of Carl August Buchholz's tract was *Über die Aufnahme der jüdischen Glaubensgenossen zum Bürgerrecht* [Lübeck, 1814]). Buchholz was a hero of the movement for emancipation; see the many references to him in the writings of Ewald (see note 158 above). See also Hilde Spiel, *Fanny von Anheim* (as in note 128), pp. 294-96, 300.

had written an ode in praise of Emperor Joseph II of Austria when the latter reversed the anti-Jewish policies of his mother, Maria Theresa, and granted some civil rights to his Jewish subjects in 1782.[167] In view of his close association with the Veit brothers and the Schlegels, Overbeck must also have known of Friedrich Schlegel's energetic response to a pamphlet by a Lübeck senator justifying his city's decision to expel the Jews.[168] Finally, the fate of Catholics could be seen as bound up with that of the Jews. As Austrian representative to the Bundestag in Frankfurt, Friedrich Schlegel vigorously criticized the Frankfurt city authorities for violating the clauses of the Treaty of Vienna that were designed to guarantee basic civil rights to both Jews and Catholics.[169]

As we saw in the correspondence of Overbeck and Johannes Veit at the time of the former's conversion, the conversion of a Jew, for Overbeck, was not essentially different from the conversion of a misguided (i.e., Protestant) or merely formal "Christian." Both he and Veit, in his view, had been moved by the same spirit. For both, as artists and as human beings, conversion had marked the beginning of a *vita nuova*. Overbeck continued to regard conversion in this light and to behave accordingly. Along with various Protestants, in whose spiritual well-being he took an interest and whom he guided along the road to conversion, there were also at least three Jews. One, a Giuseppe Arco from Ancona requested that Overbeck be his godfather when he converted in 1843.[170] Another, Ascoli by name, also from Ancona, figures in the curious

---

[167]"An den Kaiser" in Klopstock's *Sämmtliche Werke*, 10 vols. (Leipzig: Göschen, 1854), 4:262-63:

> Wen fasst des Mitleids Schauer nicht, wenn er sieht,
> Wie unser Pöbel Kanaans Volk entmenscht!
> Und tuth der's nicht, weil unsre Fürsten
> Sie in zu eiserne Fessel schmieden?
>
> Du lösest ihnen, Retter, die rostige,
> Engangelegte Fessel vom wunden Arm;
> Sie fühlen's, glauben's kaum. So lange
> Hat's um die Elenden hergeklirret.

[Who is not moved by a shudder of pity when he sees how our rabble treats the people of the land of Canaan as less than human. And do they not do so because our princes lock them (the Jews) up in iron chains? You, savior, remove the rusty, tightly fitted chains from their aching arms. They feel it and can scarcely believe it. The poor wretches have heard the clanking of chains for so long.]

[168]*Kritische Friedrich Schlegel Ausgabe*, 21:352. The senator claims, Schlegel wrote, that "die Lübecker haben *sich selbst* von dem Französischen Joch befreit, und seyen also in dieser Hinsicht nicht schuldig von den Alliierten sich Bedingungen [concerning emancipation of the Jews] vorschreiben zu lassen. Die Juden bürgerlich zu verbessern, sey *unmöglich;* dabei wird es den Juden sehr zum Vorwurf gemacht, dass sie *Hülfe von aussen* (den Schutz der Alliierten und Bundes Mächte) gegen die Unterdrückung gesucht. Den Umstand, dass die Juden zu Lübeck in dem Freiheitskriege gleich den andern Bürgern mitgedient, und eine Anzahl von ihnen auf dem Felde geblieben sind, übergeht der Verfasser weislich mit Stillschweigen." ["The Lübeckers *freed theselves* from the French yoke and are therefore not obligated to accept conditions (concerning emancipation of the Jews) that the Allies would impose on them. It is *impossible* to make the Jews into better citizens; in addition, the Jews are reproached with having sought help from outside in combatting oppression (from the Allies and the powers of the German Confederation or *Bund*). Wisely, the author passes over in silence the fact that the Jews of Lübeck served in the War of Liberation just like the other citizens and that a number of them fell on the field of battle."]

[169]In a report dated January 30, 1816. See Max J. Kohler, "Jewish Rights at the Congress of Vienna" (as in note 161), p. 76; *Kritische Friedrich Schlegel Ausgabe*, 21: 353-54.

[170]Howitt, 2:50.

incident recounted at the beginning of this essay. A third, Wolf Rinald (1785-1860), was the son of a Jewish merchant from Kassel, Josef Itzig Rinald, and his wife, Brendel Israel. As a youth, Rinald had hoped to become an artist. Pforr had become friendly with him when both were students at the Academy in Kassel. Subsequently Rinald followed Pforr to the Vienna Academy and it was there that he also formed a friendship with Overbeck.[171] When his father fell ill, however, he had to leave the Academy and give up his artistic aspirations in order to take over the family business. Overbeck must have stayed in touch with him, for in the summer of 1860 he apparently knew that Rinald was seriously ill. In July, only a few months before his former fellow-student's death, he wrote, still addressing him as "Du," to urge him earnestly to convert.[172]

In so far as the Sulamith of the *Sulamith und Maria* drawings can be seen as a figure to whom Maria is offering love and encouragement, it seems not unreasonable to interpret her, in accordance with traditional commentaries on the figure in the Song of Songs, as the soul – of Jew or Christian – in need of and yearning for love, grace, and reunion with the divine. The significance of Overbeck's original identification with the Sulamith figure can only have deepened and grown richer along with the range of his experience.

[171]In the report on his studies in Vienna, which Pforr prepared for his guardian, the merchant Sarasin of Frankfurt, he confesses that Rinald was so fulsome in his praise of Overbeck when he came to the Vienna Academy, that he (Pforr) became jealous; see Howitt, 1:79.

[172]For the text of Overbeck's letter, see Howitt, 2: 42-44.

VII

The choice by Overbeck and Pforr of two female figures to represent them has already been touched upon but deserves a brief further comment. Representations of female friendship and sisterly love were increasingly common in the late eighteenth and early nineteenth centuries and were understandably popular with women painters, such as Angelika Kauffmann, Ludovike Simanowiz, and Louise Seidler[173] **(Pf. 49-53)**. It is hard to imagine, however, that the artist who thought of his art as "a harp of David, on which I would wish endlessly to play psalms in praise of the Lord"[174] could have intended his portrayal of the two sisters Sulamith and Maria to have only a human, sentimental value, as some scholars appear to imply.[175] The relation of the Sulamith und Maria drawings and paintings to the series representing Raphael and Dürer as brother artists in the service of faith points to one level of allegorical meaning, as already suggested. But the most common female couple in the iconography of Western art is that of Synagoga et Ecclesia, the older and the younger sister, the rejected and the new bride. At times, albeit within the constraints of the *Concordia veteris et novi testamenti*, Synagoga was understood as having her place in the divine plan of redemption. St. Paul presents Hagar and Sarah, the rejected and the legitimate wife, as prefigurations of Synagoga and Ecclesia (Galatians, 4:21-30), thus leaving room for the former, though cast out, to benefit ultimately from divine compassion. For St. Justin in the second century it is Leah the "tender-eyed," with her weak vision, who is a prefiguration of Synagoga, whereas Rachel prefigures Ecclesia. St. Augustine associates Synagoga with Sarah and Ecclesia with Rebecca. In the first half of the ninth

[173]An earlier example – before 1739 – is *Lady Henrietta and Lady Elizabeth Finch* by the Irish painter Charles Jervas at Kenwood House in London.

[174]See note 2.

[175]E.g. Bettina Baumgärtel, *Angelika Kauffmann (1741-1807). Bedingungen weiblicher Kreativität in der Malerei des 18. Jahrhunderts* (Weinheim and Basel: Beltz Verlag, 1990), pp. 185-209, at p. 193: "In the second half of the 18th Century, the model of two women seated side by side and closely linked to each other became the prototype of the friendship painting in general. This continued into the Romantic era. The best known of the later works in this manner is Overbeck's 'Italia und Germania.' " This view is endorsed by Bärbel Kovalevski in her commentary on a painting by Louise Seidler in *Zwischen Ideal und Wirklichkeit: Künstlerinnen der Goethe-Zeit zwischen 1750 und 1850*, B. Kovalevski, ed. (n.p.n.d., Verlag Gord Hatje), p. 135.

century Rabanus Maurus picks up St. Paul's association of Synagoga with Hagar and Ecclesia with Sarah and adds his own: Synagoga as Naomi and Ecclesia as Ruth. In the ivories, prayer books, and lectionaries of the Carolingian period especially, Synagoga is frequently depicted as equal in status to Ecclesia **(Figs. XVI, XVII, Pf. 54)**.[176] This vision of Synagoga as a partner of Ecclesia in the divine plan for Mankind, rather than a hateful or diabolical enemy recurs in the twelfth and thirteenth centuries (the time of the commentaries on the Song of Songs by Williram and Giles of Rome), possibly as a response by the Church to the teachings of the heretical Cathari and Waldenses, who rejected much of the Old Testament. In the stained-glass "Anagogic" window of the Chapel of Saint Peregrinus at the Abbaye de Saint-Denis outside Paris, for instance, Abbot Suger had the arms of the Christ figure extend protectively over both Ecclesia and Synagoga. In addition, the latter's blindfold has been removed in accordance with Paul's prediction in II Corinthians, 3:13-16. Though standing apart from Ecclesia and still wearing the blindfold characteristic of later representations, Synagoga is portrayed in the sculptural decoration of the cathedrals of Strasbourg and Bamberg as a dignified, beautiful, and sad figure, evoking compassion rather than hatred and contempt.[177] At all times, however, other, less benign representations of Synagoga were also to be found. Even at Strasbourg and Bamberg, realistic scenes of violent attacks on Jews – real, contemporary Jews, recognizable by their Jews' hat – were depicted below the

---

[176]Why God cast out Synagoga and chose a new Bride, why He rejected the Jews and turned to the Gentiles is a mystery, according to Gregory the Great (540-604), and for that reason His incomprehensible will must be respected and not made an object of discussion. (See Ohly, *Schriften zur Mittelalterlichen Bedeutungsforschung* [as in note 72], p. 316.)

[177]On the general theological background, see Hans Liebesschütz, *Synagoge und Ecclesia: Religionsgeschichtliche Studien über die Auseinandersetzung der Kirche und dem Judentum im Hochmittelalter* (Heidelberg: Lambert Schneider, 1983, published from the author's Nachlass; the author having fled Germany in 1935 and finished the manuscript in exile) and the classic work of James Parkes, *The Conflict of the Church and the Synagogue: A Study in the Origins of Anti-Semitism* (London: Socino Press, 1934). On the changing imagery in relation to developments within the Church and in christology and on the increasing demonization of Synagoga and the Jews that accompanied the passage from the early Carolingian *Christus triumphator*, victorious over death and evil, in whom Charlemagne saw the source of his own imperial authority, to the later *crucifixus dolorosus* and the emphasis on the ritual of the mass and on the Eucharist as the body and blood of Christ, see Herbert Jochum, "Ecclesia et Synagoga. Materialien zu einer ikonographischen Christologie," *Kirche und Israel*, 7 [1992]: 171-90. On the iconography of Ecclesia et Synagoga, see also Bernard Blumenkranz, *Juden und Judentum in der Mittelalterlichen Kunst* (Stuttgart: W. Kohlhammer, 1965); Franz Böhmisch, "Exegetische Wurzeln antijudaistischer Motive in der christlichen Kunst" (as in note 70); Fathers Arthur Martin and Charles Cahier: *Mélanges d'archéologie, d'histoire et de littérature*, 4 vols. (Paris: Mme Veuve Poussielgue-Rusand, 1847-65), vol. 2 (1851), pp. 50-59; Alfred Raddetz, "Ecclesia et Synagoge" in *Judentum im Mittelalter*, Exhibition Catalogue, Schloss Halbturm, May-October 1978, Kurt Schubert, ed., pp. 109-111; Konrad Schilling, ed., *Monumenta Judaica: 2000 Jahre Geschichte und Kultur der Juden am Rhein* (Exhibition Catalog, Cologne, 1963), 2 vols., especially vol. 1 (Handbuch), pp. 152-59; Petra Schöner, *Judenbilder im deutschen Einblattdruck der Renaissance* (Baden-Baden: Valentin Körner, 2002), especially ch. 4; Heinz Schreckenberg, *The Jews in Christian Art*, trans.from the German (London: S.C.M. Press, 1996); Wolfgang S. Seiferth, *Synagogue and Church in the Middle Ages* (as in note 71); and the pioneering study of Paul Weber, *Geistliches Schauspiel und Kirchliche Kunst in ihrem Verhältnis erläutert an einer Ikonographie der Kirche und Synagoge* (Stuttgart: Ebner & Seubert [Paul Neff], 1894).

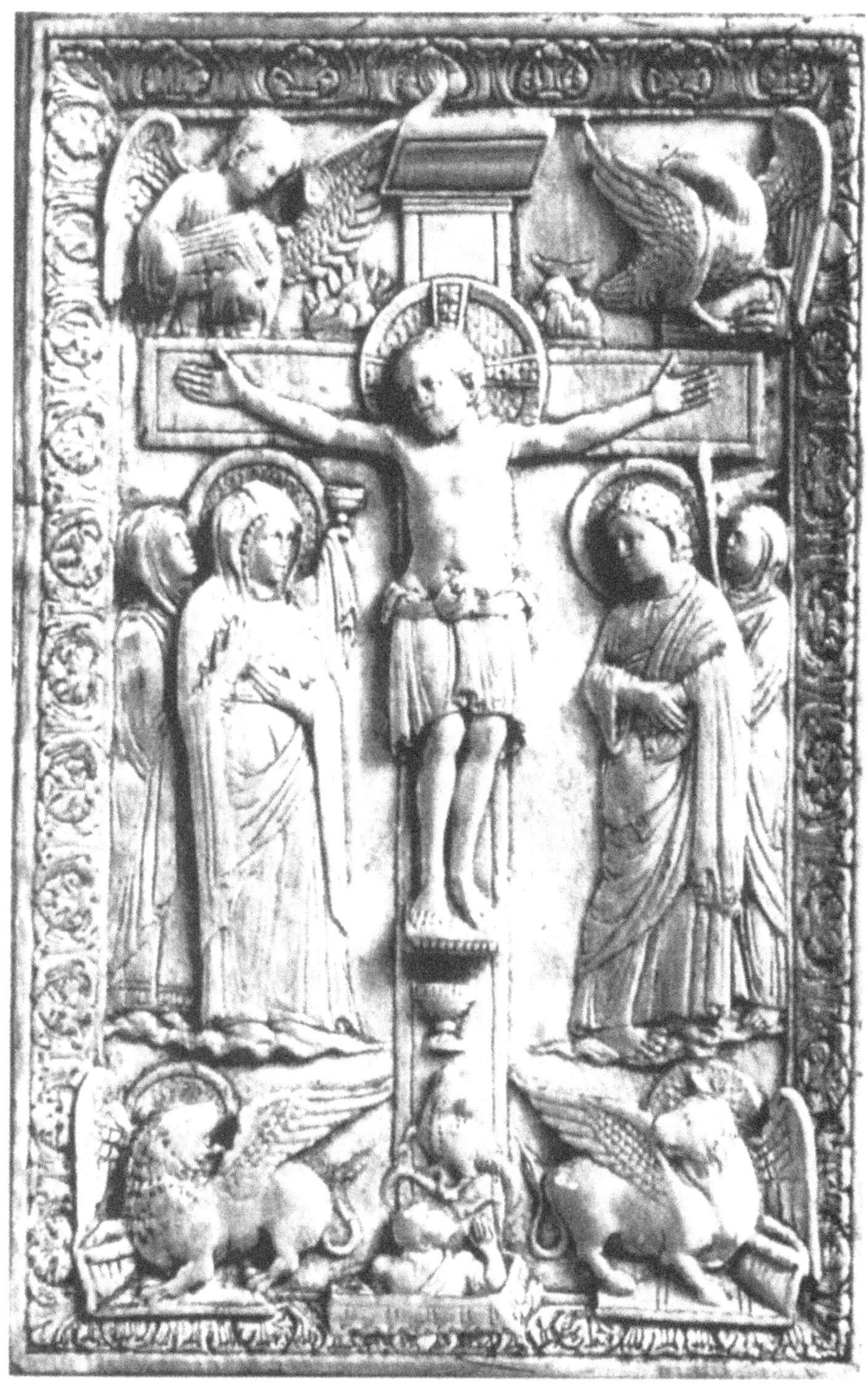

Fig. XVI. *Ecclesia and Synagoga.* Ivory relief from cover of an evangeliary, Cologne, St. George, (mid-11th Century). Darmstadt Landesmuseum, Inv. No. KG54.210b.

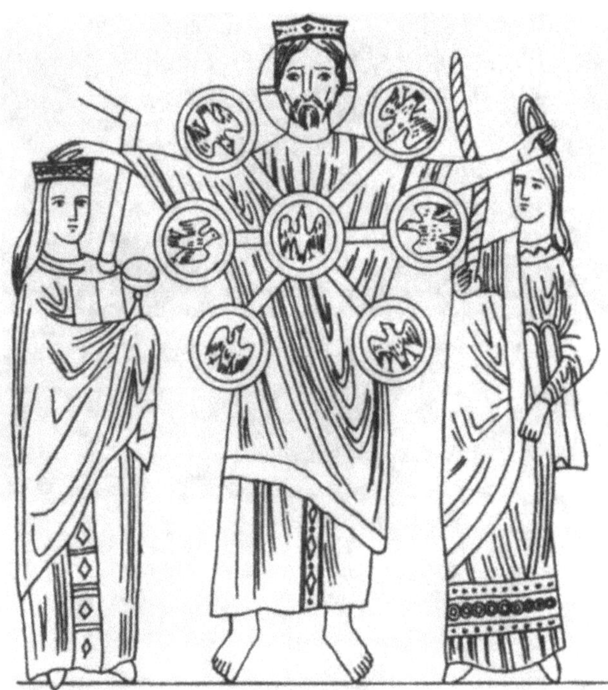

Fig. XVII. *Ecclesia and Synagoga.* Drawn from the stained-glass "Anagogic" window, Chapel of Saint Peregrinus, Abbaye de Saint-Denis. (12th Century). From illustration in Louisa Twining, *Symbols and Emblems of Early and Mediaeval Christian Art* (London: Longman, Brown, Green and Longmans, 1852), Plate XXVII. The arms of the Christ figure extend protectively over both Ecclesia and Synagoga. The latter's blindfold has been removed in accordance with the prediction in II Corinthians, 3:13-16. The abbot, Suger, may have been responding to images such as one in the *Liber floridus* of Canon Lambert of St. Bertin at Saint-Omer (circa 1100), which represents Christ violently pushing Synagoga away from him and toppling her crown (as prefigured in Lamentations, 5:16-17: "The crown is fallen from our head: woe unto us that we have sinned! For this our heart is faint; for these things our eyes are dim.")

noble figure of Synagoga.[178] By the fourteenth century hate-filled images of Synagoga, showing her humiliation or punishment as Ecclesia triumphs over her were widespread **(Figs. XVIII – XX, Pf. 55, 56)**.

It is hard to imagine that Overbeck was unaware of the iconography of Synagoga and Ecclesia and it would be surprising if no thought of it occured to him as he worked on his own two female figures for the *Sulamith und Maria* sketches and subsequently on the oil painting known as *Italia und Germania*,

[178]Herbert Jochum (as in note 176) shows that even in the Carolingian period respectful representation of Synagoga was by no means universal. On the realistic scenes of violent attacks on Jews at Strasbourg (where they are now missing but have been reconstructed from earlier drawings) and at Bamberg, see Helga Sciurie, "Ecclesia und Synagoge an den Domen zu Strassburg, Bamberg, Magdeburg und Erfurt. Körpersprächliche Wandlungen im gestalterischen Kontext," *Wiener Jahrbuch für Kunstgeschichte*, 56/57 (1993/94): 679-87.

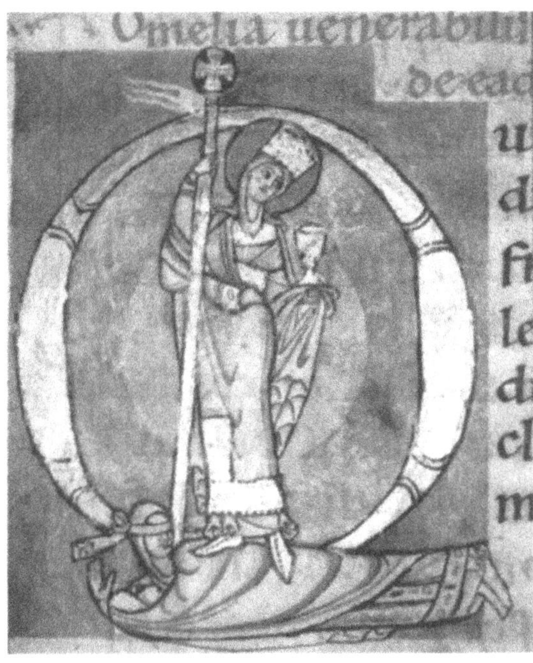

Fig. XVIII. *Ecclesia and Synagoga.* (12th Century). Verdun Cathedral, Ms. 121 (probably from Trier), folio 273 verso. From illustration in *Trésors d'un Millénaire: Dix Siècles d'art et d'histoire autour de la Cathédrale de Verdun*, exhibition catalogue, Claire Ben Lakhdar-Kreuwen, ed. (Verdun: Association Culturelle de la Cathédrale de Verdun et de la Ville de Verdun, 1990), Plate III.

in which the series of sketches culminated. The bridal crown of myrtle worn by the Maria (Germania) figure, for instance, would seem to identify her as the Bride of Christ, Ecclesia, whereas the downcast gaze of Sulamith is a feature of many representations of Synagoga. At the same time, since a downcast gaze, as a sign of modesty, is also found in images of the Virgin, it effectively adds to the suggestion of a rapprochement and fundamental identity of the two sisters. (Curiously, in his double portrait of Overbeck and Johannes Veit, Philipp Veit attributes the same downcast gaze to his brother, the converted Jew.) It seems not implausible to speculate, therefore, that one in a range of allegorical meanings suggested by the sketches and the painting – several of which have been evoked in the course of this essay – might well be that of fair-haired Ecclesia (the New Testament Maria) lovingly encouraging her dark-haired, dejected but dignified older sister, Synagoga (the "black but comely" Old Testament Sulamith) to join with her in following what Overbeck must have deemed her true path. Such a vision of the relation of Synagoga and Ecclesia, Jews and Christians, would be different from many, if not most traditional representations. It would be fully consistent, however, not only with the most

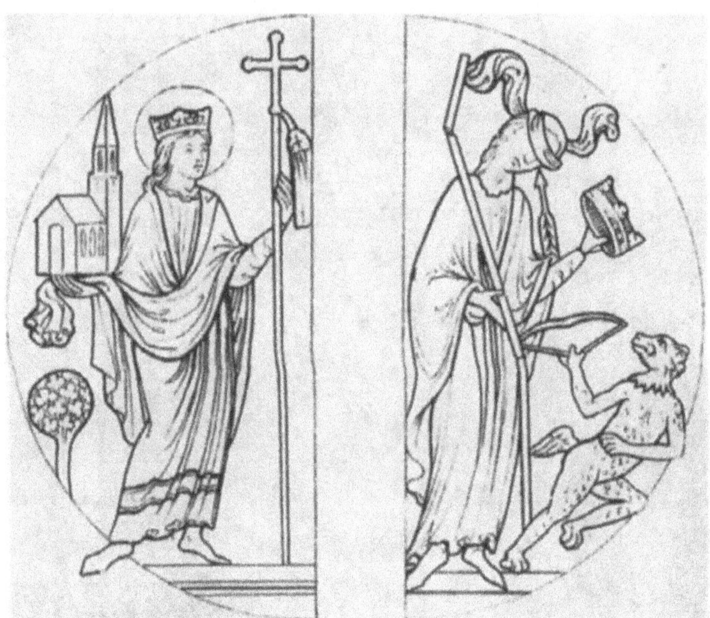

Fig. XIX. *Ecclesia and Synagoga. Chartres.* (13th Century). Drawn from stained-glass window at Chartres Cathedral. From illustration in Paul Weber, *Geistliches Schauspiel und kirchliche Kunst in ihrem Verhältnis erläutert an einer Ikonographie der Kirche und Synagoge* (Stuttgart: Ebner & Seubert [Paul Neff], 1894), p. 88. A similar stained-glass image at Cathedral of Bourges; see fine color illustration in Fathers Arthur Martin and Charles Cahier, *Monographie de la Cathédrale de Bourges, 1ère partie, Vitraux du XIIIème siècle* (Paris: Poussielgue-Rusand, 1841-44), Plate 1.

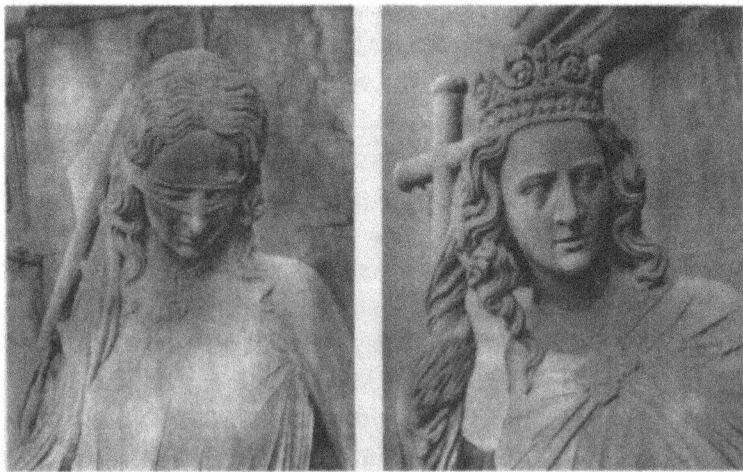

Fig. XX. *Synagoga and Ecclesia.* Strasbourg Cathedral. (13th Century). From illustrations in Otto Schmitt, *Gotische Skulpturen des Strassburger Münsters*, 2 vols. (Frankfurt a. M.: Frankfurter Verlagsanstalt, 1924), vol. 1, Plates 7 (Ecclesia) and 9 (Synagoga).

generous traditional Christian attitude toward the Jews (that they should be treated as older brothers, with charity and consideration, so that they will be moved in their hearts to convert, and thus prepare the way for the coming of the Heavenly Jerusalem) but with Overbeck's larger vision of seeming opposites as "not separate or exclusive of each other" but "joined in a beautiful and deeply felt friendship, . . . in harmony and mutual respect."

Appendix

Select Bibliography of Works on the Nazarenes, Arranged Chronologically

Works in English

1882 – J. Bevington Atkinson, *Overbeck* (London: Sampson Low, Marston, Searle, & Rivington; New York: Scribner and Welford). Illustrated Biographies of the Great Artists series.

1964 – Keith Andrews, *The Nazarenes: A Brotherhood of German Painters* (Oxford: Clarendon Press). This work includes an excellent bibliography.

1978 – William Vaughan, *Romantic Art* (London: Thames and Hudson).

1979 – William Vaughan, *German Romanticism and English Art* (New Haven, CT: and London: Yale University Press).

1980 – William Vaughan, *German Romantic Painting* (New Haven, CT: and London: Yale University Press).

2000 – Cordula Grewe, "The Invention of the Secular Devotional Picture," *Word and Image*, 16: 45-57.

2001 – Mitchell B. Frank, *German Romantic Painting Redefined: Nazarene Tradition and the Narratives of Romanticism* (Aldershot, UK: Ashgate).

2002 – Mitchell B. Frank, " 'Castrated Raphael': Friedrich Overbeck and allegory." *Word & Image,* 18, no. 1: 87-98.

2003 – Lionel Gossman, "Unwilling Moderns: the Nazarene Painters of the Nineteenth Century," *(www.19thc.artworldwide.org/autumn_c3/articles/goss.shtml)*

2004 – Cordula Grewe, "Beyond Hegel's End of Art: Schadow's Mignon and the Religious Project of Late Romanticism," *Modern Intellectual History*, 1, no. 2: 1-33.

2005 – Cordula Grewe, "Reenchantment as Artistic Practice: Strategies of Emulation in German Romantic Art and Theory," *New German Critique*, Winter issue, 36-71.

WORKS IN GERMAN

General Studies of the Nazarene Painters and Their School

1928 – W. Neuss, "Das Wesen der Nazarenerkunst und ihre Bedeutung für die deutsche Kunst des 19. Jahrhunderts," *Kunstwissenschaftliches Jahrbuch der Görresgesellschaft*, ed. J. Sauer, 1. Jahrgang (Augsburg: Dr. Benno Filser), pp. 62-86.

1977 – *Die Nazarener*, Exhibition Catalogue, Städelsches Institut, Frankfurt am Main, April-August 1977, Klaus Gallwitz, ed. (Frankfurt am Main: Städtische Galerie im Städelschen Institut). Contains many valuable essays.

1981 – *Die Nazarener in Rom: Ein deutscher Künstlerbund der Romantik*, Exhibition Catalogue, Galeria Nazionale d'Arte Moderna, Rome, January-March 1981, Klaus Gallwitz, ed. (Rome: De Luca; Munich: Prestel). Likewise contains important contributions from German and Italian scholars.

1982 – Herbert Schindler, *Romantischer Geist und christliche Kunst im 19. Jahrhundert* (Regensburg: F. Pustet).

1989 – Manfred Jauslin, *Die gescheiterte Kulturrevolution* (Munich: Scaneg).

1992 – Gudrun Jansen, *Die Nazarenerbewegung im Kontext der Katholischen Restauration* [chiefly on Clemens Brentano and Edward von Steinle] (Essen: Die blaue Eule).

2000 – Sabine Fastert, *Die Entdeckung des Mittelalters. Geschichtsrezeption in der nazarenischen Malerei des frühen 19. Jahrhunderts* (Munich and Berlin: Deutscher Kunstverlag).

2000 – Cordula Grewe, "Historie ohne Handlung: Zur Transzendierung von Zeitlichkeit und Geschichte" in *Kunst/Geschichte: zwischen historischer Reflexion und ästhetischer Distanz*, Gotz Pochat and Brigitte Wagner, eds. (Graz: Akademische Druck- und Verlagsanstalt).

2001 – Wilhelm Schlink, "Heilsgeschichte in der Malerei der Nazarener," *Aurora: Jahrbuch der Eichendorff-Gesellschaft*, no. 61 (Stuttgart: Jan Thorbacke), pp. 97-118.

2005 – Max Hollein and Christa Steinle, *Religion macht Kunst: die Nazarener* (Cologne: Verlag der Buchhandlung Walther König). (Regrettably, this important work appeared after the present essay had been completed.)

2006 – Cordula Grewe, "Italia und Germania: Zur Konstruktion religiöser Seherfahrung in der Kunst der Nazarener," in Paolo Chiarini and Walter Hinderer, eds. *Rome-Europa: Treffpunkt der Kulturen 1780-1820* (Würzburg: Könighausen & Neumann), pp. 401-26. (Regrettably, this article appeared after the present essay had been completed.)

Studies Centered on Individual Nazarene Artists

1870 – Hermann Riegel, *Cornelius, der Meister der deutschen Malerei* (Hannover: C. Rümpler).

1886 – Margaret Howitt, *Friedrich Overbeck. Sein Leben und Schaffen*, 2 vols., Franz Binder, ed. (Freiburg: Herder; rprt. Bern: Herbert Lang, 1971).

1901 – Martin Spahn, *Philipp Veit* (Bielefeld und Leipzig: Velhagen & Klasing). Künstler-Monographien, 51.

1904 – Friedrich Haack, *M. Von Schwind* (Bielefeld und Leipzig: Velhagen & Klasing). Künstler-Monographien, 31.

1905 – David Koch, *Peter Cornelius. Ein deutscher Mahler* (Stuttgart: J.F. Steinkopf).

1906 – Christian Eckert, *Peter Cornelius* (Bielefeld and Leipzig: Velhagen & Klasing). Künstler-Monographien, 82.

1911 – Hans Wolfgang Singer, *Julius Schnorr von Carolsfeld* (Bielefeld and Leipzig: Velhagen & Klasing). Künstler-Monographien, 103.

1914 – Käthe Brodnitz, *Nazarener und Romantiker: Eine Studie zu Friedrich Overbeck* (Berlin: Emil Ebering). Kunstgeschichtliche Studien, Heft II.

1915 – W.L. von Lütgendorff, *Das Overbeckzimmer im Museum am Dom in Lübeck* (Lübeck: Gebrüder Borschers).

1924 – Fritz Herbert Lehr, *Die Blütezeit romantischer Bildkunst: Franz Pforr, der Meister des Lukasbundes* (Marburg: Verlag des kunstgeschichtlichen Seminars der Universität Marburg an der Lahn).

1928 – Kurt Karl Eberlein, *Die Malerei der deutschen Romantik und Nazarener im besonderen Overbecks und seines Kreises* (Munich: Kurt Wolff).

1938 – Ludwig Grote, *Die Brüder Olivier und die deutsche Romantik* (Berlin: Rembrandt-Verlag).

1943 – Werner Teupser, *Italia und Germania, zwei Gemälde der deutschen Frühromantik, Pforr und Overbeck* (Berlin: Gebrüder Mann).

1963 – Jens Christian Jensen, *Friedrich Overbeck. Die Werke im Behnhaus* (Lübecker Museumshefte, Heft 4).

1972 – Ludwig Grote, *Joseph Sutter und der nazarenische Gedanke* (Munich: Prestel).

1980 – Frank Büttner, *Peter Cornelius: Fresken und Freskenprojekte*, vol. 1 (Wiesbaden: Franz Steiner). (Vol. 2 followed in 1999.)

1985 – Béla Hassforther, *Das Gemälde "Sulamith und Maria" von Franz Pforr*, M.A. thesis, Kunsthistorisches Institut Heidelberg (www.bela1996.de/art/pforr).

1989 – *Johann Friedrich Overbeck 1789-1869. Zur zweihundertsten Wiederkehr seines Geburtstages.* Exhibition Catalogue, Museum für Kunst und Kulturgeschichte der Hansestadt Lübeck, June-September Andreas Blühm and Gerhard Kerkens, eds. (Lübeck: Museum für Kunst und Kulturgeschichte).

1991 – Norbert Suhr, *Philipp Veit (1793-1877). Leben und Werk eines Nazareners: Monographie und Werkverzeichnis* (Weinheim: V.C.H.).

1994 – *Julius Schnorr von Carolsfeld 1794-1872*. Exhibition Catalogue, Museum der bildenden Küste, Leipzig, March – May, Herwig Guratzsch, ed. (Leipzig: Edition Leipzig).

1994 – *Julius Schnorr von Carolsfeld. Aus dem Leben Karls des Grossen. Kartons für die Wandbilder der Münchner Residenz.* Exhibition Catalogue, Stephan Seeliger, ed. (Munich: Prestel).

1994 – *Julius Schnorr von Carolsfeld. Zeichnungen*, Exhibition Catalogue, Landsmuseum Mainz, november 1994 – January 1995, Norbert Suhr and Stephan Seeliger, eds. (Munich: Prestel).

1996 – Gerde-Helfe Vogel, ed., *Julius Schnorr von Carolsfeld und die Kunst der Romantik* (Greifswald: Steinbecker Verlag Ulrich Rose).

1999 – Cordula Grewe, "Die Klugen und Törichten Jungfrauen: Wilhelm von Schadows Parabeln auf konfessionelle Versöhnung und soziale Fürsorge, 1835-1842," *Pantheon*, 57: 127-50.

1999 – Brigitte Heise, *Johann Friedrich Overbeck: Das künstlerische Werk und seine literarischen und biographischen Quellen* (Cologne/ Weimar/ Vienna: Böhlau).

2001 – Michael Teichmann, *Julius Schnorr von Carolsfeld. Monographie und Werkverzeichnis* (Frankfurt/Berlin/Bern/Bruxelles/New York/Oxford/Vienna: Peter Lang).

2002 – *Johann Friedrich Overbeck: Italia und Germania*, Exhibition Catalogue, Neue Pinakothek, Munich, February-April (Munich: Kulturstiftung der Länder, 2002; Patrimonia series 224).

The Nazarenes in General Histories of Nineteenth-Century German Art

1893-94 – Richard Muther, *Geschichte der Malerei im 19. Jahrhundert*, 3 vols. (Munich: G. Hirth), vol. 1. (Engl, trans.: *History of Modern Painting*, 4 vols., revised ed. [London: J.M. Dent / New York: E.P. Dutton, 1907], vol. 1.)

1899 – Cornelius Gurlitt, *Die deutsche Kunst des Neunzehnten Jahrhunderts* (Berlin: Georg Bondi).

1904 – Julius Meier-Graefe, *Entwicklungsgeschichte der modernen Kunst*, 3 vols. (Stuttgart: Jul. Hoffmann).

1909 – Karl Scheffler, *Deutsche Maler und Zeichner im neunzehnten Jahrhundert* (Leipzig: Insel Verlag).

1911 – Heinrich Wölfflin, *Kunstgeschichte des 19. Jahrhunderts. Akademische Vorlesung* [given at University of Berlin, 1911], Norbert Schautz, ed. (Alfter: Verlag und Datenbank für Geisteswissenschaften, 1993).

1925 – Gustav Pauli, *Die Kunst des Klassizismus und der Romantik* (Berlin: Propyläen Verlag).

1926 – W. Kurth, *Deutsche Maler im 19. Jahrhundert* (Berlin: Die Buchgemeinde).

1927 – Karl Scheffler, *Die europäische Kunst im neunzehnten Jahrhundert. Malerei und Plastik*, 2 vols. (Berlin: Bruno Cassirer), vol. 1: *Geschichte der europäischen Malerei vom Klassizismus zum Impressionismus.*

1939 – Richard Benz and Arthur von Schneider, *Die Kunst der deutschen Romantik* (Munich: Piper Verlag).

1966 – Ludwig Grote. *Klassizismus und Romantik in Deutschland. Gemälde und Zeichnungen aus der Sammlung Georg Schäfer, Schweinfurt.* Exhibition Catalogue, Germanisches Nationalmuseum, Nuremberg.

1970 – Ludwig Grote, *Beiträge zur Motivkunde des neunzehnten Jahrhunderts.* Munich: Prestel).

1976 – Hans-Joachim Neidhardt, *Die Malerei der Romantik in Dresden* (Leipzig: VEB/E.A. Seeman Verlag).

1978 – Herbert von Einem, *Deutsche Malerei des Klassizismus und der Romantik 1760 bis 1840* (Munich: C.H. Beck).

1984 – Willi Geismeier, *Die Malerei der deutschen Romantik* (Dresden: VEB Verlag der Kunst).

1985 – *Deutsche Romantiker: Bildthemen der Zeit von 1800 bis 1850,* Exhibition Catlaogue, Kunsthalle der Hypokulturstiftung, Munich, June – September Christoph Heilmann, ed. (Munich: Hirmer Verlag).

1988 – Helmut Börsch-Supan, *Die deutsche Malerei von Anton Graff bis Hans von Marées 1760-1870* (Munich: C.H. Beck / Deutscher Kunstverlag).

2005 – Hubert Locher, *Deutsche Malerei im 19. Jahrhundert* (Darmstadt: Wissenschaftliche Buchgesellschaft / Primus Verlag).

Index of Proper Names

www.ingramcontent.com/pod-product-compliance
Lightning Source LLC
LaVergne TN
LVHW081601100826
845153LV00004B/429

* 9 7 8 0 8 7 1 6 9 9 7 5 6 *